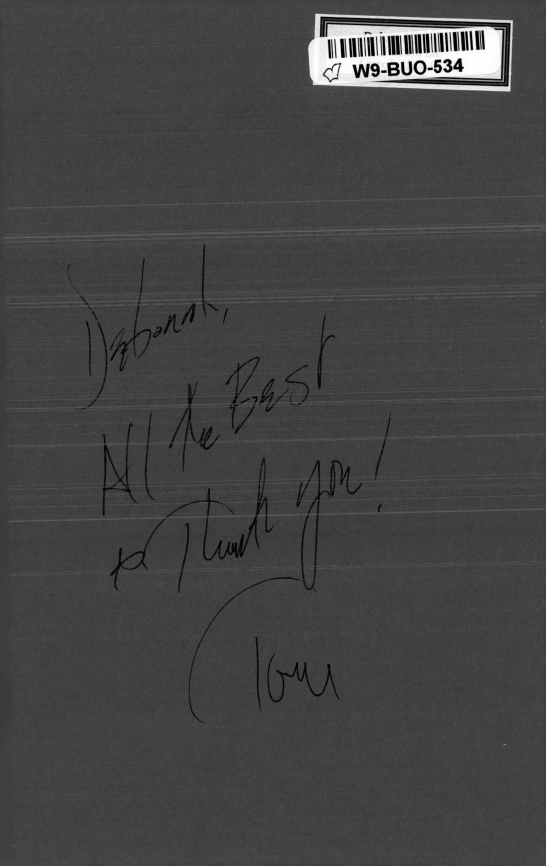

Deborah,

All the Best

& Thank you!

Tom

Writing the Breakthrough Business Book

The Ultimate Guide for Consultants,
Entrepreneurs, Executives, Experts, and Writers

Writing
the
Break
Through
Business
Book

Tom Gorman

Content Publishing

The table of contents of the *Seven Habits of Highly Effective People*, copyright ©1998 by Stephen R. Covey, is used with the permission of Franklin Covey Company, which owns the trademark on each of the Seven Habits.

Fry's Readability Graph, copyright ©1985 by the International Reading Association, is reprinted with the permission of Edward B. Fry and the International Reading Association. All rights reserved. Reference: *Classroom Strategies for Secondary Reading, 2nd Ed.*, W. John Hawker (Ed.), International Reading Association, chapter 8, 50-62.

The proposal for *Business Is a Contact Sport*, copyright ©2000 by Tom Richardson and Augusto Vidaurreta, is used with the permission of the authors.

Cover and interior design by Pneuma Books, LLC
For more information, visit www.pneumabooks.com

Disclaimer: This book is intended to provide general information on writing and book publishing. It is not meant to be the reader's only source of information on these subjects, and readers are urged to seek advice from other sources, some of which are listed in Appendix 2 of this volume, and to use their own judgment.

This book contains the ideas and opinions of the author and is sold and distributed with the understanding that the author and publisher are not dispensing legal, consulting, or other professional services in the book. It is also sold and distributed with the understanding that the information in this book is current only to the time it was written and that, while every effort has been made to ensure the information is accurate, mistakes in content and presentation may have occurred.

Therefore the author and publisher disclaim any responsibility for any liability, loss, or risk incurred as a direct or indirect consequence of the use or application of any of the contents of this book.

Publisher's Cataloging-in-Publication
(*Provided by Quality Books, Inc.*)

Gorman, Tom.
    Writing the breatkthrough business book : the ultimate guide for consultants, entrepreneurs, executives, experts, and writers / Tom Gorman
    p. cm.
    Includes bibliographical references and index.
    LCCN 2002095451
    ISBN 0-9724426-0-X
    1. Business writing   I. Title.

HF5718.3.G672003   808'.06665
                  QBI02-200837

10 09 08 07 06 05 04 03   5 4 3 2 1

Dedicated to readers of business books,
and to the authors, editors, agents, and other
publishing professionals who serve them.

Table of Contents

Acknowledgments

One of the greatest assets anyone undertaking a new endeavor can have is a mentor and coach who has deep knowledge and experience and the willingness to share them. Literary agent Mike Snell of the Michael Snell Literary Agency in Truro, Massachusetts has been that kind of guide to me and to hundreds of other business book authors. After ten years of writing books, I still learn something new in every conversation I have with Mike. This book could not have been written without him.

Nor could it have been written without my clients, who have taught me as much about writing and collaboration as they have about their areas of expertise. These include Dr. Paul Miller of the Miller Institute, Mike Hruby of Technology Marketing Group, Tom Richardson and Augusto Vidaurreta of RAM Technologies, and those clients who wish to remain unidentified. Thank you for sharing your ideas and experiences with me, and for letting me be part of your creative pursuits.

Thanks also go to Peter Lowy, Todd Domke, and Brian Tarcy for their insightful comments on drafts of the manuscript, to Kate Layzer for another superb editing job, and to Brian Taylor, Michael Morris, and their talented team at Pneuma Books for their design and production work. Anita Halton generously shared her first-hand knowledge of business book promotion with me.

As always, thank you Phyllis, Danny, and Matthew for supporting my every effort in the risky but rewarding world of book publishing.

Introduction

As a full-time business book author, I meet many consultants, entrepreneurs, and executives who think there is a book in their business. Whether they are right or wrong—and they are often right—many of these men and women have spent months or years writing unsalable book proposals or manuscripts before seeking help or even charting a path to their goal. Others have spent good money to have bad material developed by writers who lack experience with business books. I've written this book for those business people and those writers, and for anyone who wants to avoid their mistakes.

In other words, if you are a business person who wants to write a book or have one written and published, you have found the right guide. If you are a professional or aspiring writer who wants to break into the lucrative business book genre—as an author or a ghostwriter—you have also found the right guide.

This book is written for:

- Consultants, entrepreneurs, executives, and experts who want to write a business book or want to work well with a collaborator or ghostwriter (the latter being an uncredited collaborator)
- Professional writers and aspiring authors who want to write their own business books, work on them as collaborators, or just improve their business book proposals, manuscripts, and promotional efforts
- Agents, editors, and other publishing professionals who want a guide to the business book genre for their own use or to offer to clients, colleagues, and authors.

Business titles now represent a substantial segment of book publishing, as well as a mature literary genre. Over 1,500 business books are published annually, according to Christopher Murray, editor-in-chief at Soundview Executive Book Summaries. Entire publishing houses, as well as imprints within publishing empires, are dedicated to business books.

This market thrives because people care about their jobs, careers, and finances. They read business books because they want money, status, security, good working relationships, and self-fulfillment. Most business people have a strong need to succeed, and success depends on knowledge, skill, and the ability get things done through others. Fear also motivates readers. People want to avoid job loss, bankruptcy, bad investments, downward mobility, and embarrassment in the workplace. They also want to keep up with a business world that changes at least as often and quickly as any other aspect of their lives. These motivations ensure that business books will continue as a popular publishing genre.

I mention this because economic and political developments in the United States have taken a turn that no one could have anticipated at the height of the late 1990s economic boom. The stock-market meltdown, downturn in the business cycle and, most significantly and tragically, terrorist attacks and subsequent developments have left the United States and its business community in a state of uncertainty, in contrast to the boundless optimism of a few years ago.

We have witnessed a turning point, and turning points leave book publishers in a quandary. What, exactly, should they publish? During an expansion, business books become optimistic, even irrationally exuberant, in tone. Frothy titles and "management-lite" books abound. In a recession, nuts-and-bolts titles move to the fore. Although the economic cycle will have progressed by the time you read this, as of this writing US business people and the authors, agents, editors, and publishers who produce books for them have retrenched and become reflective. We all want to avoid mistakes, preserve what we have, and process what has occurred.

This processing takes time, and that favors the book business. Despite its adoption of digital technology, book publishing remains a somewhat quaint enterprise. Most editors must still think at least a year ahead when they sign a book. Authors think even further into the future. Meanwhile, television runs round the clock. Newspapers arrive on our doorsteps every morning. Movies invade the multiplexes every Friday. Magazines hit the newsstands every month. In this context, an author taking a year to write a book possesses all the modernity of a frock-coated counting house scribe. But the sheer time and thought involved in writing a book can bring forth a way of looking at the world that literally changes that world.

In 1972, *What Color Is Your Parachute?* began changing people's views of the job hunt, the job market, and the job itself—and they never changed back. The early 1980s recession saw the publication of *In Search of Excellence*, which changed the way managers saw their companies and their role in them. In 1990 and the decade that followed, readers discovered *The Seven Habits of Highly Effective People* and started seeing themselves in a new light in relation to their colleagues, customers, families, and friends.

These breakthrough books reached millions of readers, but many less popular books also generate breakthroughs. A single reader, if he is the right reader with the right book at the right time, will experience a breakthrough—to new knowledge, new skills, or a new point of view—if the author has done her job well. The author does her job well when she develops her message to its fullest potential, then tries to take it further. If she succeeds, she breaks through to new territory, heightening the likelihood that her readers will too. For that author and her readers, that book is a breakthrough book.

Four Issues for Everyone

Four issues warrant mention before you read *Writing the Breakthrough Business Book*:

First, this book deals primarily, but not solely, with business how-to books. As Chapter 1 explains, this includes books on many subjects—leadership, job hunting, marketing, investing, strategy, quality control, and a broad range of executive and business skills. Narratives about companies, executives, or business events are another category of business books. The process of getting published is quite similar for business narratives and business how-to books, but this book focuses a bit more on the latter.

Second, business book publishing works on a two-tier system. On the top tier are celebrity-CEOs and famous entrepreneurs, and those who collaborate on their books—usually writers from the *Wall Street Journal* and the major business magazines. This book is written for everyone else. Neither Jack Welch, the former chairman of GE, nor John Byrne, a senior writer at *Business Week* and Welch's collaborator on *Jack: Straight from the Gut,* needed to worry about getting an agent, writing a detailed book proposal, or persuading an editor to give them a contract and a multimillion dollar advance. So throughout this book, much of the advice could be qualified with the phrase, "unless you are a celebrity-CEO or famous entrepreneur."

Third, this book deals mainly with the traditional publishing process rather than electronic- or self-publishing. Although Web-based publishing may help authors and companies build links to customers, almost all readers still prefer hard-copy books for lengthy works. (E-books, for example, have so far failed to find a large market.) Self-publishing works well for many business book authors, and much of this book applies equally to self-published and traditionally published authors. But the process of self-publishing is complex and covered thoroughly in other books. (See Appendix 2.)

Finally, I write business books for a living and view writing them as a business endeavor. Therefore, this book covers not only writing issues but also business matters such as finding an agent who handles business books, weighing offers from publishers, and reviewing book contracts. Lack of business skill has scuttled as many writing careers as lack of writing skill.

A Word to Writers

From the working writer's perspective, business books offer a realistic path into book publishing. While it's true that major publishers favor authors with a "platform"—fame, followers, seminars, or some other means of promoting or selling books—new, unknown authors break in all the time, even at the major houses. What's more, the consultant, entrepreneur, or executive who wants to have a book developed or written typically needs the help of a professional wordsmith. That translates into ample opportunities for writers who are willing and able to collaborate on business books for a fee, a share of the advance and royalties, or both.

However, to write a business book, particularly as a collaborator, an author needs some knowledge of business. If you are already a writer working in a business, or have business experience, you are ahead of the game. If not, you can learn about business through books, magazines, newspapers, and courses. At the outset, you must pick your projects and market yourself carefully. Writing a book about job hunting for a small publisher will be a more realistic undertaking than writing one on leadership for a large publisher. To become established, seek straightforward book projects and some smaller projects, such as magazine articles or editing work, and charge competitive rates. Then, work your way up with each succeeding project.

A Word to Consultants, Entrepreneurs, and Executives

Writing the Breakthrough Business Book aims to serve two audiences equally well—professional and aspiring writers, and business people who want to get a book published, whether they write it or hire a writer. Most business people new to book publishing find themselves amazed or annoyed by aspects of the industry, such as its relatively slow pace and arcane decision-making procedures. Many business people are shocked by the amount of work it takes to develop, write, publish, and promote a book, even with a collaborator on board.

If you're a business person, this book will help you understand the industry and the process, avoid most problems, and speak (or at least comprehend) the language. It will help you set ambitious but realistic goals for a book project and then reach those goals.

Above all, it will show you how to convert your passion into a publishable book. This book provides practical advice on getting published, yet it is no substitute for genuine enthusiasm for your subject. Choose a topic you love. Make your message memorable. Try to change your readers' lives. Passion and enthusiasm will carry you a long way through this process and will ratchet up the quality of your book.

The Structure of This Book

- Chapter 1—The Business Book Bonanza—examines business books and the categories within the genre and explains the paths to publication.
- Chapter 2—Developing the Breakthrough Book Idea—reveals ways of coming up with exciting ideas and titles for business books and creatively positioning them in the market.
- Chapter 3—The Fast Track to a Book Deal—discusses ways of finding an agent and a publisher.
- Chapter 4—Business Book Proposals that Sell the Sizzle—shows how to write a business book proposal that gets agents and editors excited.
- Chapter 5—Sample Material Editors Can't Resist—focuses on creating a table of contents, chapter summaries, and a sample chapter that convince an editor to make an offer on your book.
- Chapter 6—Sixty Thousand Sparkling Words—shows how to present material and write in ways that will keep the reader engaged and entertained as he's being informed.
- Chapter 7—The Manuscript Is Finished, But the Project Isn't—describes the editorial and production process, flags potential problems, and suggests solutions.
- Chapter 8—Tell the World about Your Book and Your Business—explores the how-to of book promotion, which plays

a critical role in the success of business titles. This chapter also shows how to use a book to promote your business.

- Appendix 1 presents a business book proposal that sold to Alpha Books.
- Appendix 2 provides resources for business book writers and for anyone who wants to learn more about specific aspects of book publishing.
- The Glossary explains common book publishing terms.

The goal in writing a breakthrough book is to transcend the genre of business book. Much of the fun and fascination in the project lies in pursuing that transcendence. The best business books take their subject—whatever it is—as the context for showing readers what any first-rate book of any genre shows them: how to improve their lives while improving the lives of others. When a book does that, genuine breakthroughs occur.

The Business Book Bonanza

Understanding the Market and Deciding Where You Fit

 usiness books have become a major genre in publishing only in the past twenty years, but their history is as long as that of modern management. Both management and books about management arguably began with the 1911 publication of *The Principles of Scientific Management* by operations analyst Frederick W. Taylor. (Of course, if published today, the book's title would be *10 Principles of Super-Successful Management*). Business thinker Peter Drucker issued his groundbreaking study of General Motors, *Concept of the Corporation*, in 1946 and went on to write more than a dozen serious management books. For decades he was the only "business book author" most managers could name, aside from Dale Carnegie.

Dale Carnegie launched the business how-to category with *How to Win Friends and Influence People* in 1937. With more than fifteen million copies in print, his book remains a landmark sixty-five years later. Oilman J. Paul Getty—a billionaire back when a billion was real money—wrote *How to Be Rich* in the early 1960s. First serialized in *Playboy* and published in book form in 1965, *How to Be Rich* was one of the earliest celebrity-CEO books.

Even before the 1980s—the decade that made success our national obsession—business books regularly achieved popularity and occasionally hit the best-seller lists. *Business as a Game* by Albert Carr, published in 1968, sold well. In 1969, Lawrence Peter's wildly popular *The Peter Principle* explained, as the subtitle promised, "why things go wrong." (Answer: Managers are promoted until they reach a job they cannot do. Thus "in a hierarchy, everyone rises to his level of incompetence.") In the early 1970s, sales of *Power: How to Get It, How to Use It* by Michael Korda and the irresistibly titled *Winning through Intimidation* by Robert Ringer skyrocketed. The irreverent management guide *Up the Organization* by Avis CEO Robert Townsend flew out of stores. In 1973, Alan Lakein's *How to Get Control of Your Time and Life* focused readers on their to-do lists. Three years later, James Molloy's *Dress for Success* put them into sack suits. In 1977, *The Gamesman: The New Corporate Leaders* by Michael Maccoby identified four basic types of managers—the Craftsman, Organizational Man, Jungle Fighter, and Gamesman, the last being a new type of corporate player, perhaps one who had read Carr's *Business as a Game*.

For decades, books on "evergreen" topics such as job hunting and investing had produced respectable and occasionally spectacular sales. Witness the success of *What Color Is Your Parachute?* by Richard Nelson Bolles, which has been revised annually since 1972 and has sold over 22 million copies worldwide. Several inspirational business titles, such as the proto-New-Age *Think and Grow Rich* by Napoleon Hill, also produced for their publishers.

Yet despite such successes, the business genre amounted to a book publishing backwater until the 1980s. What made publishers get down to business books?

Money, of course.

In Search of Sales

For a product category to take off, two things must exist: the right product and the right market. Despite the success of some business titles up to then, the business book market as we know it didn't emerge until the 1980s. In that decade, the economy shook off the stagflation of the 1970s, the nation focused on business, and we entered an age of glitzy prosperity. People hungered for success and its trappings. Hollywood responded with *Dallas* and *Dynasty* on television and *Wall Street* on the big screen. Pop music went corporate. The baby boomers got real jobs, lost the weird threads (see *Dress for Success* above), and replaced MBA for LSD as a generational rite of passage.

Into this potpourri landed two breakthrough books: *In Search of Excellence* and *The One Minute Manager.* Each of them, in its own way, altered business people's book-buying behavior.

Penned by McKinsey consultants Tom Peters and Bob Waterman, *In Search of Excellence* kicked business books to a new level. Published in hardcover in 1982, this was a true management book directed to working managers. It was not "about" selling or interviewing or dressing. It didn't cover a single company or celebrity-CEO. Nor was it too dry or too fluffy. The book took a new, though not revolutionary, approach. Part journalism, part academic research, and a lot of well-expressed opinion from two savvy consultants, it examined what made *companies* successful and distilled those factors into eight principles. Though *Search* was not an immediate hit, it soon became *the* book to have read. It focused on large companies, like those then being overrun by baby boomers, and it spoke about achieving organizational rather than individual success. Thanks partly to some companies' buying it in bulk—a harbinger of the future—more than three million copies were in print twenty years later.

Over that same period, *The One Minute Manager* more than doubled that sales figure. Written in a simple storybook format by Kenneth Blanchard and Spencer Johnson, this eighty-page book's common-sense approach to communication demystified management for many readers. (Fifteen years later, Johnson would demystify change for millions more readers with *Who Moved My Cheese?*) If *In Search of Excellence* was meant to demolish command-and-control practices (as Tom Peters says it was), then *The One Minute Manager* was an instruction book for the guy or gal who was actually managing by wandering around, a technique found in *In Search of Excellence*.

Both of these books tapped managers' newly discovered hunger for knowledge, skills, and techniques that would give themselves and their companies an edge. Publishers stepped up to meet that demand. Today, a business book can appeal to—and win—millions of readers. This is particularly true of breakthrough business books.

Break on Through

A breakthrough is a new approach, trend, or development. A breakthrough business book introduces a new approach, trend, or development to readers. The book may or may not be a best seller. The idea of the book may or may not be a breakthrough idea, at least at first. But a business book author should approach every idea he develops and every book he undertakes as a potential breakthrough. That attitude inspires creativity. It encourages the author to build up the idea of the book, make it exciting, and present it uniquely. Often the presentation is what generates the breakthrough.

While most business books inhabit a genre, an author should never see her book as generic. She should see it as transcending its genre. Consider the following breakthrough books and their genres and subjects:

- *The Millionaire Next Door* is a personal-finance book that says habits of managing money, rather than a high income, represent the path to wealth.
- *Guerrilla Marketing* is a marketing book that shows how to get big results on a small budget.
- *The Seven Habits of Highly Effective People* is a how-to-succeed book that stresses principled management and self-management.
- *Competitive Advantage* is a strategy book that explains that a company must understand its value chain and excel at the activities in that chain.
- *Management and the New Science* is a management book that applies principles of quantum physics to organizations and markets.
- *Getting to Yes* is a book on how to negotiate that says focus on interests rather than positions and seek win-win solutions.

As the next chapter will show, a simple idea underlies each of these books. But that idea was well developed and presented in a way that promised something people want. Often the idea, and the element that lifts the book above others in its genre, is contrary to previous expectations or presents something familiar in a new light. *Millionaire* refutes the notion that millionaires all have huge salaries. *Guerrilla Marketing* says that a creative David can beat a big-budget Goliath. *Competitive Advantage* introduced the idea of the value chain, while *Management and the New Science* looked at management through a new lens. *Getting to Yes* recommends not playing hardball in negotiations, which is the natural tendency of many business people.

What else can make a breakthrough book?

Being the first to use a method of presentation can do the trick. For instance, Wess Roberts' *Leadership Secrets of Attila the Hun*, published in 1989, was a breakthrough book. Al Kaltman's entertaining *Cigars, Whiskey and Winning: Leadership Lessons from Ulysses S. Grant*, published in 1998, was not. By then too many books on historical figures' leadership secrets had been done. But a decade earlier, *Attila* was so fresh and appealing that it actually launched the "Leadership-Secrets-of . . ." subgenre.

Firmly grounding the book in research or an intellectually rigorous approach can create a breakthrough. In business books, substance (often) sells. *The Millionaire Next Door* by Thomas Stanley and William Danko and *Leadership IQ* by Emmett Murphy, both based on years of research, made the best-seller lists. Throughout the 1990s, Michael Porter's *Competitive Strategy* and *Competitive Advantage* sold briskly, as did other serious but accessible books by his colleagues at Harvard and other business schools.

Positioning an idea for a broader audience can enable a book to transcend its genre and break through. Stephen Covey, who specializes in principle-based leadership, had written books and consulted with companies well before writing *Seven Habits*. However, Jan Miller, the very creative agent who represented that book, helped Covey position his ideas for virtually everyone. Who doesn't want to be an effective person?

Not every business book can become a breakthrough book, but that is what every author should aim to create. If you fall short, you'll still bring forth the best book that was in you, and probably outrun the competition in the category.

A Field Guide to Business Book Genres

As we will see, you must position your book effectively—first, in your own mind and then in the minds of others—in order to land an agent and a publisher. You may believe that your book is unique and beyond category. It could be, but that's not the way to bet. Agents and editors connect with material they like, but they also think of books as products and the first thing they look at is the proposed book's genre.

Remember, we are considering only true business books, not business biographies (such as *Titan: The Life of John D. Rockefeller Sr.* by Ron Chernow) or humor (such as Scott Adams' Dilbert books), even though these appear on the *New York Times* Business Best Sellers list. Much can be learned from the lives of industrial titans, and, clearly, Dilbert does mirror much of corporate life. But here we define business books more narrowly.

Business book genres fall into two broad categories: business how-to/self-help books and books about companies, people, trends, and events.

Business how-to/self-help books are the meat-and-potatoes of business books. Name a business skill—from advertising to zero defects—and titles have been published on it. How-to/self-help covers so much ground that subgenres on specific skills have sprung up, such as books on interviewing skills, which fall within the job hunting genre. Sample titles include *101 Great Answers to the Toughest Interview Questions* by Ron Fry, *Five Top Secrets to Getting More Money in a Job Interview* by Michael W. Hall, and *Power Interviews: Job-Winning Tactics from Fortune 500 Recruiters* by Neil Yeager and Lee Hough.

Books about companies, people, trends, and events cover most titles outside the how-to/self-help categories. These books range from serious journalism and narrative nonfiction to puff pieces about or by celebrity-CEOs.

The Book Buying Decision

As in most consumer purchases, a mix of practical and emotional factors affects readers' book buying decisions. At the practical level, business how-to/self-help buyers want to acquire a skill, solve a problem, improve their performance, prepare for a new role, compete more effectively, or otherwise enhance their professional standing and increase their earnings. They also want to be entertained. If they didn't, they would buy a workbook, textbook, or manual on the subject. At the emotional level, these readers want to assuage their fears, increase their confidence, enhance their prestige, or gain a psychological edge over competitors.

Readers of books about companies, people, trends, and events also want to learn, but they are not driven to acquire skills. They want to see business people in action and witness the inner workings of a company or personality. They also want a good read. At the practical level, these readers want to stay abreast of events and get the "inside story." They want to be able to discuss the topic in business and social situations. At the emotional level, they want to identify with those they admire, gloat over the misfortunes of others, feel like insiders, and respond viscerally to the subject.

Although there is some cross-over of subject matter and mingling of reader motives between these two broad categories—how-to/self-help and books about companies, people, trends, and events—it's best to think of them as separate.

Business How-to/Self-help

The lists below do not include every genre of business book, and they name only a few representative titles within each genre. But they do provide an overview of the business book landscape.

Executive and Managerial Skills

Executive and managerial skills books target managers at all levels as well as aspirants to those positions. Books have been published on virtually every executive and managerial skill imaginable, including:

- thinking and planning
- conducting meetings
- hiring and keeping good employees
- organizing paper, projects, and people
- appraising performance
- firing and laying off people
- acting like an executive
- communicating
- dressing like an executive

Numerous books have also been published on:
- financial management
- marketing management
- HR management
- product development
- managing turnarounds

Among the genres covering specific skills are the following:

Leadership

An extremely popular category over the past ten years, leadership books appeal to those who want to improve their executive persona, managerial thinking, motivational skills, and organizational cultures. Popular titles include:
- *First Break All the Rules: What the World's Greatest Managers Do Differently* by Marcus Buckingham and Curt Coffman
- *Good to Great: Why Some Companies Make the Leap and Others Don't* by James C. Collins
- *Servant Leadership* by Robert K. Greenleaf
- *Deep Change: Discovering the Leader Within* by Robert E. Quinn
- *The Contrarian's Guide to Leadership* by Stephen Sample and Warren Bennis

As noted, "Leadership-Secrets-of..." books achieved widespread popularity, although the fad has currently faded:

- *Leadership Secrets of Colin Powell* by Oren Harari
- *Leadership Secrets of Elizabeth I* by Shaun O'L. Higgins and Pamela Gilberd
- *Jesus CEO* by Laurie Beth Jones

Change Management

The business environment of the past twenty years has created a lively market for books on managing organizational change:

- *Leading Change* by John P. Kotter
- *Journey to the Emerald City* by Roger Connors and Tom Smith
- *The Change Monster* by Jeanie Daniel Duck
- *Making Six Sigma Last: Managing the Balance between Cultural and Technical Change* by George Eckes
- *The Dance of Change* by Peter M. Senge

Creating Customer Relationships

Books on CRM (customer relationship management) could be viewed as a subset of books on selling, but they are not. CRM books typically view customers from a higher altitude—some might say a safer distance—and comprise their own genre. They deal with policies and behaviors that create customer satisfaction:

- *The Loyalty Effect* by Frederick F. Reichheld
- *Customer Loyalty: How to Earn It, How to Keep It* by Jill Griffin
- *Customer Retention* by Michael W. Lowenstein
- *Performance Driven CRM* by Stanley A. Brown and Moosha Gulycz
- *The Customer-Centered Enterprise* by Harvey Thompson

Teams and Team Building

The books-on-teams genre has grown over the past decade, driven by the 1990s trend toward leaner, flatter organizations and cross-functional approaches to work:

- *The Wisdom of Teams* by Jon R. Katzenbach and Douglas K. Smith
- *Body and Soul: Unleashing the Power of Your Team* by Bob Gernon
- *Leading Self-Directed Work Teams* by Kimball Fisher
- *The 17 Indisputable Laws of Teamwork* by John C. Maxwell
- *Global Teams* by Michael J. Marquardt and Lisa Horvath

Strategy Books

The success of Michael Porter's books intensified publishers' focus on the subject of strategy:

- *20/20 Foresight: Crafting Strategy in an Uncertain World* by Hugh Courtney
- *Co-opetition* by Adam M. Brandenburger and Barry J. Nalebuff
- *Evolve: Succeeding in the Digital Culture of Tomorrow* by Rosabeth Moss Kanter
- *Judo Strategy* by David B. Yoffie and Mary Kwak
- *Blown to Bits: How the Economics of Information Transforms Strategy* by Philip Evans and Thomas S. Wurster

Other How-to/Self-Help Categories

Books on skills and other topics for those outside the managerial ranks also abound, as do books for managers in special situations.

Sales & Selling

Some publishers avoid books on selling because they don't see salespeople as big readers. Nevertheless, certain books in the genre have sold quite well, including the following, which range from the fundamental to the sophisticated to the inspirational:

- *How to Master the Art of Selling* by Tom Hopkins
- *Solution Selling: Creating Buyers in Difficult Selling Markets* by Michael T. Bosworth
- *The New Strategic Selling* by Stephen E. Heiman, et al.
- *The Greatest Salesman in the World* by Og Mandino

The following subjects within selling have also been covered:
- personal, face-to-face selling
- getting to the right person
- direct marketing
- sales presentation skills
- telemarketing
- closing skills

Job Hunting

When people lose their jobs, they become quite needy quite suddenly. They need information, encouragement, and support, and many of them turn to books for it:
- *10 Insider Secrets to Job-Hunting Success* by Todd Bermont
- *Knock 'Em Dead* by Martin Yate
- *Don't Send a Resume and Other Contrarian Rules to Help Land a Great Job* by Jeffrey J. Fox
- *Post Office Jobs: How to Get a Job with the U.S. Postal Service* by Dennis V. Damp

Career Management

With the employer-employee social contract in tatters and diminished loyalty on both sides of the desk, career management has become a dependable genre. Most of these books don't cover job hunting in much depth. Instead, they help readers cope with office politics, enhance promotability, handle relationships, make wise career moves, and deal with career crises:

- *Rites of Passage at $100,000 to $1 Million* by John Lucht
- *The Pathfinder: How to Choose or Change Your Career for a Lifetime of Satisfaction and Success* by Nicholas Lore
- *Laid Off & Loving It!* by Paul David Madsen
- *What Your Boss Doesn't Tell You Until It's Too Late: How to Correct Behavior that is Holding You Back* by Robert M. Bramson

Small Business and Entrepreneurship

Although small business management could be considered a managerial skill, the subject has fostered its own genre. Books targeting readers in the SOHO (small-office/home-office) market encompass the full range of skills needed to establish and build a home-based business or a small firm:

- *The Successful Business Plan: Secrets & Strategies* by Rhonda M. Abrams and Eugene Kliener; *Successful Business Planning in 30 Days* by Peter J. Patsula
- *Starting on a Shoestring* by Arnold S. Goldstein; *What No One Ever Tells You about Starting Your Own Business* by Jan Norman
- *Poised for Growth: Taking Your Business to the Next Level* by Gabor Baumann; *Big Vision, Small Business: Four Keys to Success without Growing Big* by Jamie S. Walters
- *Financial Troubleshooting: An Action Plan for Money Management in Small & Growing Businesses* by David H. Bangs Jr. and Michael Pellecchia; *Simplified Small Business Accounting* by Daniel Sitarz

Personal Finance Books and Guides to Investing

Two things set personal finance and investing books apart from other business books. First, they speak to readers in their off-the-job roles as investors, homeowners, debtors, parents, and retirees. Second, most of the authors are financial planners, investment counselors, or money managers. This genre is so specialized and successful that many large publishers have editors who handle these books almost exclusively. A few smaller houses focus heavily or exclusively on these books.

General personal finance books cover the subject broadly and include topics such as saving, budgeting, getting out of debt, and understanding your attitudes toward money. They tend to cover investing in the context of an overall personal financial strategy:

- *Rich Dad, Poor Dad: What the Rich Tell Their Kids About Money that the Poor and Middle Class Do Not!* by Robert T. Kiyosaki
- *The Road to Wealth* by Suze Orman
- *Your Money Matters: 21 Tips for Achieving Financial Security in the 21st Century* by Jonathan Pond
- *Multiple Streams of Income* by Robert G. Allen

Narrowly targeted personal finance books also find a market:

- *Miserly Moms: Living on One Income in a Two-Income Economy* by Jonni McCoy
- *Complete Idiot's Guide to Money for Teens* by Susan Shelly
- *Become Totally Debt-Free in Five Years or Less* by Gwendolyn D. Gabriel, et al.
- *The Best Way to Save for College* by Joseph F. Hurley.

Books on investing, as opposed to personal finance, focus solely on investing and mainly on the stock market:

- *The Only Investment Guide You'll Ever Need* by Andrew Tobias
- *One Up on Wall Street* by Peter Lynch
- *Investing for Cowards* by Fred Siegel

Other books on investing cover specialized strategies, skills, and securities:

- *The Disciplined Trader: Developing Winning Attitudes* by Mark Douglas

- *The Art of Short Selling* by Kathryn F. Staley
- *The 16% Solution: How to Get High Interest Rates in a Low Interest World with Tax Lien Certificates* by Joel S. Moskowitz

And then there are books on real estate investing, a category that boomed with the 1980 publication of the breakthrough book *Nothing Down* by Robert G. Allen (which has sold more than 1,250,000 copies):

- *Value Investing in Real Estate* by Gary W. Eldred
- *How to Find Real Estate Bargains* by Robert Irwin
- *Rental Houses for the Successful Small Investor* by Suzanne P. Thomas
- *Flipping Properties* by William Bronchick and Robert Dahlstrom
- *How to Make Money in Commercial Real Estate* by Nicholas Masters

Books about Companies, People, Trends, and Events

Well-known and even not so well-known companies, people, trends, and events regularly generate books. These are narrative, rather than instructional, in tone and sometimes represent breakthroughs.

Books on Companies

Authorized books about companies come from the CEO, usually in as-told-to form, or are written by an outsider with the company's cooperation. They aim to tell the company's success story or to set the record straight, and often overlap with the celebrity-CEO genre. Unauthorized books, written without the company's cooperation, often take a balanced or even complimentary approach to their subject:

- *Only the Paranoid Survive* by Andrew S. Grove (Intel's CEO)
- *Pour Your Heart into It: How Starbuck's Built a Company One*

Cup at a Time by Howard Schultz (Starbuck's CEO) and Dori Jones Yang
- *The Weather Channel* by Frank Batten (CEO of Landmark Communications, owner of the Weather Channel) with Jeffrey L. Cruikshank
- *IBM Redux: Lou Gerstner and the Business Turnaround of the Decade* by Doug Garr
- *Inside the Magic Kingdom: Seven Keys to Disney's Success* by Thomas K. Connellan
- *McDonald's: Behind the Arches* by John F. Love

Business Exposé

The author Dorothy Parker said, "If you haven't got anything nice to say, sit next to me." Some publishers share this sentiment and issue uncomplimentary books, or outright exposés, about celebrity-CEOs or companies. Many of these books fall short of serious journalism, relying instead on old news, disgruntled sources, and one-sided reporting. However, others embody serious journalism.

- *Just Desserts: The Unauthorized Biography of Martha Stewart* by Jerry Oppenheimer
- *The Operator: David Geffen Builds, Buys and Sells the New Hollywood* by Tom King
- *Chainsaw: The Notorious Career of Al Dunlop in the Era of Profit-At-Any-Price* by John A. Byrne
- *When Genius Failed: The Rise and Fall of Long-Term Capital Management* by Roger Lowenstein
- *Barbarians at the Gate: The Fall of RJR Nabisco* by Bryan Burrough and John Helyar

Celebrity-CEO Books

Written by the executive or in as-told-to form, these books set forth the trials, tribulations, achievements, and wisdom of their author. Then-Chrysler-CEO Lee Iacocca invigorated this genre with his best-selling 1984 book *Iacocca*, written with William Novak. The best of these books capture the executive's "voice" on paper and include some, though hardly all, warts. If the CEO lacks candor, humor, and storytelling skill, these types of books can be as exciting to read as the Uniform Commercial Code. Done well, they can be quite entertaining.

- *Work In Progress* by Michael Eisner with Tony Schwartz
- *The Art of the Deal* by Donald Trump with Tony Schwartz
- *Sam Walton: Made In America* by Sam Walton with John Huey
- *A Passion to Win* by Sumner Redstone with Peter Knobler
- *Losing My Virginity* by Richard Branson

Business Trends and Events

Most book publishers try to recognize and exploit societal trends. Similarly, successful business book editors and authors monitor business trends and try to capitalize on them. Books can also reinforce management fads—teams and reengineering spring to mind—but at their best, they help readers cope with or profit from business developments. Thus some books in this category overlap with the how-to genre.

The biggest trends of the 1990s—the World Wide Web and the raging bull market—spawned scores of titles. While books that blatantly exploit red-hot trends rarely become backlist favorites (want to buy a copy of *Dow 36,000*?), they can rack up big sales before the trend fades. Some titles covering a business trend or event do prove more durable:

- *Free Agent Nation* by Daniel H. Pink
- *The Entertainment Economy* by Michael J. Wolf
- *Blur: The Speed of Change in the Connected Economy* by Stan M. Davis and Christopher Meyer

- *Facing Up to Management Faddism: A New Look at an Old Force* by Margaret Brindle and Peter N. Stearns

Not Elsewhere Classified

Two other types of books warrant mention: professional/technical books and corporate histories. These are not trade books—that is, books sold at popular prices through traditional and online bookstores—but they do represent a publishing option for authors and companies.

Professional/Technical Books

Professional/technical books stand about halfway between trade books and textbooks. They deliver information to working professionals, straight with no chaser. Often these books update professionals on changes in practices due to new laws, regulations, or business conditions. They do not boast glossy dust-jackets, and they are usually distributed through direct mail, catalogs, and Web sites rather than bookstores, although many are available at online booksellers. Some large trade publishers, such as McGraw-Hill, maintain professional/technical book divisions, while other houses publish them exclusively.

Accounting, human resources, and operations management generate many professional/technical books. Accounting, a complex field to begin with, constantly responds to new laws and developments. HR professionals must continually address new issues, such as diversity, sexual harassment, and compliance with the Americans with Disabilities Act. (Legal publishing is an industry unto itself, as are books on computers and software.) Operations management in manufacturing raises engineering and technical issues far too specialized for a general management audience. And that's the key to books in this category: They cover subjects for experts rather than general readers.

It's been said that generalists are an inch deep and a mile wide, while experts are a mile deep and an inch wide. Although these characterizations rarely apply to individuals, they do make a point relevant to business book authors. An author who writes for a general trade-book audience should be a generalist and write like a generalist, or write with one. An expert writing for experts should seek a professional/technical publisher.

Corporate Histories

Corporate histories don't normally reach bookstores and therefore are not trade books. But they represent a publishing option for well-established companies. These books are commissioned by the company to tell the story of its founding, growth, successes, key people, and, hopefully, failures (which add interest and credibility). Often published to celebrate a major anniversary year, they are paid for by the company and distributed to employees, investors, customers, and other stakeholders.

While the company does pay to have them published, they are not *per se* vanity books issued by subsidy (or vanity) publishers. A few small U.S. publishers, such as Greenwich Publishing Group, develop and produce well designed, properly edited, high-quality corporate histories. These books typically contain photographs and other visual memorabilia, so they are best handled by outfits that can deal with those aspects of book production.

A corporate history maximizes a company's control over the book. However, because it won't be distributed through the trade, it won't be widely read by the public. (Also, tight control by the company often results in a painfully dull book.) A corporate history is primarily just that—an historical document of the company's people, products, practices, and progress. The best of the genre also capture the spirit of the company between covers.

Successful Series: The Mother Lode

DOS for Dummies was rejected by several major publishers before it was picked up by IDG (now Hungry Minds, part of John Wiley & Sons). Those who turned it down saw the title as a nonstarter. Who'd want to be seen on the subway reading a book for dummies?

But they didn't consider the fact that DOS made everyone feel like a dummy. The title worked. It worked so well that other *Dummies* technology titles soon followed. The formula—simple prose, short sections, numerous chapters, and lots of sidebars—appealed to readers. Soon, Alpha Books introduced its parity product (okay, its knockoff) *Complete Idiot's Guides*.

The publishers noticed that sales of these books followed the cycles of software releases. To diversify, they introduced business titles, which also succeeded, and then lifestyle titles including wine, beer, classical music, and even (must we encourage their procreation?) *Sex for Dummies*. The business titles sold quite well, with the *Complete Idiot's Guide to Starting a Business* once that line's top seller.

Most business book publishers have tried to develop a popular series, and some have succeeded. Wiley & Sons spun a *Portable* series off its successful *Portable MBA*. Adams Media created a *Streetwise* series. *Guerrilla Marketing* launched a *Guerrilla* series for Houghton Mifflin.

As of this writing, the quest for successful business series continues. Editors know that a solid series can make their careers. It can also make an author's career, so be sure to consider the series potential of a book idea as part of your development process.

A Mature Product Line

Business books regularly hit the general best-seller lists and now have their own monthly list in the business section of the *New York Sunday Times*. They command their own sections in bookstores. Most major publishing houses have business divisions or imprints, and numerous smaller publishers devote all or part of their lists to business books. (See Appendix 2.)

This means that the term business book bonanza cannot be dismissed as hyperbole. According to Frank Daly, executive director of the Book Industry Study Group, based in Matawan, New Jersey, annual business book sales rose from $617 million in 1995 to over $1 billion in 2000. Although sales dipped to about $940 million in 2001 due to the recession, Daly forecasts a return to growth in 2003 and a return to the $1 billion mark in 2005. In any event, the number of business books sold annually should exceed 50 million units for the next several years, so the market remains strong.

The question is: What role do you want to play in this market?

Your Publishing Options

This book explains how to get a trade business book published. It shows how to develop a salable idea, write a book proposal, find a literary agent, land a contract, and write and promote the book. Within that model (and outside it, for that matter), there are various ways to have a book published.

Large Publishers

The pros and cons of publishing with a large house resemble those of working for a large company. You'll have more up-front money and the "prestige" of having a recognized publisher's name on the book. Most large houses also know what they are doing, in the same way that most large companies know what they are doing. That is, they have systems for getting things done, but they are not usually going to stretch themselves to new heights or handle things well if you don't fit their system. With a large publisher you get the distribution resources of a large company, if not its marketing resources.

Your book will have one "season"—about four to six months—

to find its audience and start selling. After that it is relegated to the backlist, to make room for the publisher's frontlist for the next season. Most large publishers issue new lists about every four months. They therefore have three "seasons" a year and use terms such as "the autumn list" and "the spring list" to designate the new titles. The books are issued over the months of that publishing season, rather than all at the beginning of the season.

Major publishers rely heavily on literary agents to screen material and help them judge book ideas and authors. They have to, given the volume of submissions they receive—1,000 to 2,000 a year at large business book houses, such as McGraw-Hill and Wiley & Sons. Thus an agent is almost a must for an author pursuing a major house. I say "almost" because, even at a large publisher, a truly great proposal can find its way to the right editor and prompt her to make an offer. Yet even in such cases it is preferable, especially for a new author, to have an agent negotiate the advance and contract. So it makes sense to work with an agent and have the benefit of her advice and experience from the start.

Small and Medium-Size Publishers

About a dozen large houses and imprints publish business books. So do many small to medium-size houses, some as their sole product line and some as part of their general nonfiction list. These houses receive fewer submissions, pay lower advances (as low as $1,000), and have smaller lists. Some give authors more control over their books as well as more personal attention. Virtually all of them consider unagented submissions.

Smaller publishers often tend their backlists more carefully than large houses. They try to buy books that will endure beyond the season and put relatively more resources into nurturing their backlists. But they also must battle for shelf space, so if an editor says that her house "works hard to maintain the backlist," ask for specifics.

Some small publishers use direct marketing to reach readers. For instance, Paramount Market Publishing, based in Ithaca, New York, sells books directly to marketing professionals. These include trade titles and professional/technical books. Publishers like Paramount can reach readers in specific functions, such as marketing, finance, or human resources. They are worth investigating for a book with a niche audience.

The greatest advantage of small-to-medium-size houses is that they seriously consider unagented proposals from unknown authors and books that target tens of thousands, rather than hundreds of thousands, of readers.

Professional/Technical Publishers

Again, authors covering specialized topics for small audiences should consider professional/technical publishers. Advances, when they are paid at all, tend to be quite low relative to those of trade houses, so very few agents represent material aimed at these publishers. This means that authors with professional/technical material can forgo an agent and use a shorter proposal than the one presented in this book. Try a two-to-three page description of the book, its audience, and the need it fills, a page or two about your qualifications, a table of contents, and perhaps a few sentences describing each chapter. If the publishers are interested, they will either ask for more details or a sample chapter, or they may make an offer based on your material, qualifications, and writing experience.

Incidentally, some professional/technical titles do quite well and stay in print for years by establishing a reputation and remaining current through periodic revisions.

Self-Publishing

A publisher puts up money to have the book developed, written, edited, designed, manufactured, distributed, and marketed. A self-publisher performs or outsources some or all of these tasks. To go the self-publishing route, an author must be a bit of a business person. He must also have the money to fund the publication process and the knowledge to pull it off.

Not every book is a good candidate for self-publication. Ideally, the book should fill a pressing need for useful information in a reachable audience. Fortunately, many business books fit that profile. Self-publishing makes especially good sense for the company that wants to maximize its control over a book intended mainly for employees, investors, customers, and other stakeholders.

More than a word of caution is in order. It is easy for a novice self-publisher to ignore, fudge, or "wish away" certain tasks that established publishers have learned to face squarely. These include assessing the viability of the book idea and its audience, judging the quality of the writing and design, and following through with distribution and marketing. Self-publishing a book based on a bad idea that you happen to believe in is a waste of time, effort, and money. If you cannot find a publisher for your book, *honestly* assess whether the barrier is the idea, the presentation of the idea, or the size of the target audience. If the size of the potential audience has stopped publishers from snapping up the idea and the audience is large enough for you, fine. Otherwise it's time to let go of the idea or redo the approach. Creating a trade-quality book calls for a professional writer, editor, page designer, and cover designer. The absence of one or more of these professionals on a project has resulted in many an amateurish book. Even more self-published books have been scuttled by the author's failure to master the logistics of distribution. Despite their shortcomings, established publishers do get books into stores, albeit for brief stays.

Publishers also take care of editing, design, manufacturing, and numerous invisible details that would drive many experienced authors—let alone consultants, executives, entrepreneurs, and academics—raving mad. The self-published author must address all of these issues, and the successful ones do exactly that. They learn how from other self-publishers and from the several good books that have been published (or, more accurately, self-published) on the topic. Dan Poynter's *Self-Publishing Manual* is widely considered the best starting point and has seen many a new publisher through the process. (Also see Appendix 2.)

Book publishing is as tough as any business. However, for the talented and determined author, there is always a way into print. And it all begins with an idea.

2

Developing the Breakthrough Book Idea

Finding an Idea and Creating a Title

he ideas behind most business books, and even most breakthrough business books, are fairly simple. Yet many business people make ideas needlessly complex, usually in an effort to make them seem more sophisticated or original. A good idea is usually easy to grasp. It need not be totally original, but it should give the reader a fresh approach to a business problem, skill, or situation. Or it should present the business matter in a new and different light. It is the author's approach or presentation (rather than the business matter or the idea) that is new. Approach and presentation come down to packaging the idea, which begins with the title of the book.

Agents, editors, and readers want fresh and fascinating books. The author also wants something—and before embarking on the long road to publication, he had better figure out what that is.

This chapter first examines various motives for writing a business book and then kicks off the development process, which begins with finding and refining an idea and generating a working title for the book.

Why Write a Business Book?

Business books may be the most frankly commercial genre in book publishing. After all, commerce is their subject, and the reader's motivations are largely commercial (as, of course, are the publisher's). If business books are about making money, it's only reasonable that some of it sticks to the author's toner-stained fingers. There are other good reasons for writing a business book, which we will examine, but let's start with the monetary motivations.

Make Money from the Book

Business book authors fall into three categories: authors, expert-authors, and ghostwriters. Each makes money from a book project in a different way:

- As the *author* of your own book, you make money from the advance and the royalties paid by the publisher.
- As an *expert-author*—a consultant, entrepreneur, executive, or professor who has written a book—you make money from the advance and the royalties, or a share in them. You also make money by using the book to promote your company or consulting practice, thereby increasing your sales or fees.
- As a *ghostwriter*, you make money from a share in the advance and royalties or from fees paid by an expert-author who wants to have a book written, or from a combination of the two.

Each of these three types must invest in a book. Authors and ghostwriters invest their time, and writing a book is among the most time-consuming undertakings ever devised by the human mind. Expert-authors invest their time and, almost always, money. All three also invest their skill, energy, and reputation.

A new author or expert-author will make some money, but should not plan on making a lot *on the book itself* unless he can command a huge advance or has a sure-fire platform for moving books. Here's why: For a business book by a new, unknown author, a small to mid-size publisher typically pays an advance ranging from $1,000 to $7,500. A major house will usually pay $10,000 to $40,000. Major houses will occasionally exceed this range for "newbies," but it takes an aggressive agent and a red-hot idea. The advance is paid in two or three installments: half on signing the contract and half on the publisher's acceptance of the entire manuscript; or one-third, one-third, and one-third on signing, delivery of half the manuscript, and acceptance of the entire manuscript.

Until the advance is earned back, the author receives no royalties. If the book does not earn out its advance, the author keeps the full amount, which is nice because many books do not earn out their advances. Of course, publishers are not enthusiastic about doing a second book with an author whose first book failed to earn out its advance, particularly if the advance was large.

The above ranges notwithstanding, advances for business books vary wildly depending on the book, author, agent, and publisher. Since it is impossible to predict the amount of the advance or the number of copies that will sell, you cannot know ahead of time how much a book will earn. Meanwhile, it takes work to write a proposal, which might not even find a publisher. Of course, an author could write a proposal, land an agent, get an offer, weigh the size of the advance, and *then* decide whether to write the book. A decision not to write the book, however, would probably alienate the agent who sold the proposal and would leave the author with nothing to show for his efforts.

Professional authors and ghosts realize that a career is built over time. They don't count on making big money on their first book or even their first few books. Similarly, expert-authors should not expect to make much money on the book itself. They should focus more on using the book to promote their business.

Promote a Business

Expert-authors usually write a book to boost their business, their consulting practice, their company, or their career. They correctly expect a return, in the form of higher earnings, on the time and money invested in the book. But a book will not automatically boost sales. To succeed as a marketing tool, a book must be employed like any other marketing tool, and this means answering the questions:

- What is my goal?
- Who are my prospects?
- What is my message?
- What are my alternative media?
- Which medium is best for my message?
- What are my costs?
- How do I convert prospects to customers?
- How do I measure success?

Answered honestly, these kinds of questions might reveal that a book would not be the best promotional tool for a given business. There are, of course, other good reasons for a business to have a book, such as conveying its story or principles to employees and investors. If the aim is promotion, however, then promotional issues must be considered right from the start. The book should form the thin end of a wide wedge consisting of speaking engagements, articles, newsletters, a Web site, and other tactics of an integrated marketing program.

That said, writing a book and having it published does confer the title of "author" on a person. It establishes that individual as an "expert." The credibility that comes with the publication of a book can, in and of itself, help a business person attract attention, educate prospects, and set her company apart from others of its type.

Become Famous

Too old, fat, and bald to become a rock star? Having trouble breaking into acting? Hate doing jail time? You can still achieve fame—as an author.

Pursuing fame is like promoting a business, only more difficult. Very few best-selling authors attain genuine Oh-look-there-he-is fame. Yet even without a best seller, fame may be within reach—if it's properly defined.

A striped-bass fishing friend of mine recently announced that he's "getting famous on eastern Long Island."

"Really?" I asked.

"I sometimes go to a new beach, and I meet guys I haven't met before and they already know me, they've heard of me." Then he added, "It's a pretty small world, striper guys."

Ah! Here's a man who understands the true definition of fame, which is being known to people you don't know, even if they don't number in the millions.

A business book that fails to catapult its author to international stardom can still make him famous in his world. Alan Weiss may not be a household name, but as the author of *Million Dollar Consulting: The Professional's Guide to Growing a Practice*, he is quite well known to independent consultants and regularly speaks at their gatherings. Few people would recognize Tom Hopkins, or even his name. However, many serious salespeople have read *Mastering the Art of Selling* and attended Hopkins' seminars. Have people outside the business world heard of Michael Porter or Tom Peters?

You probably have. But had you heard of them before they wrote their books?

Establish or Enhance a Writing Career

Business books are a relatively easy genre to break into. This doesn't mean it's easy, and it's downright difficult at the major houses. But relative to many nonfiction categories, business books are easier to research, write, and sell. Therefore, they offer a path into book publishing for business journalists, copywriters, securities analysts, and other industrial inkslingers. More than a few B-school professors have written trade books after toiling over academic tomes. Nonbusiness writers who can learn about business can either add business books to their repertoire or move into the genre full time.

The fastest way for a new, non-expert, garden-variety writer to break in is to collaborate with an expert-author. I wrote my first book, *Big League Business Thinking*, with Paul Miller, an executive development consultant I knew socially. No money changed hands. We simply split the advance (and the work) fifty-fifty. The book was published by Prentice Hall, earned out its advance, codified Dr. Miller's thinking, landed me an agent, and gave me experience.

Business book publishers like the combination of expert-author and professional writer. Many business people have great content but cannot write to trade-book standards. Others lack the time or patience to write a book. So opportunities for writers are out there. After you do a business book or two as a credited or uncredited collaborator, you should have the experience and credibility to write them under your own name, if you wish. A new writer can break in without a "content expert." It's just a bit harder.

Create a Product or Documentation

Business how-to books, the majority of business books published, show readers how to learn skills and solve problems. In sharing that information in book form, the author stakes a copyright-protected claim of ownership. A book codifies an author's thinking and documents her expertise. It may sum up a lifetime of work. As a tangible, respected, permanent public record, a book can support a strategy of "defensive publishing" in which publishing a concept, principle, practice, or process establishes at least primacy and often ownership. (But an author cannot own an idea, only the expression of an idea.)

Books have launched companies (*Age Wave*), boosted companies' business (*The Popcorn Report*), and established brands (*The Oz Principle*). They have accompanied, explained, and promoted products ranging from Hacky Sacks to heart rate monitors. Although an author should never count on getting rich from a book, a book is a product with a price tag, and some authors have earned huge sums in royalties. With 22 million copies of his book in print, Richard Bolles knows the color of his parachute—it's the color of money.

There are, of course, other reasons to write a business book. You may enjoy writing and love business for its drama and intellectual content. You may want to write about an aspect of business in order to learn it inside out (which works, by the way). Or you may want to help others by sharing your knowledge and experience. Perhaps you lost a bet, or your predecessor wrote a book, or you promised your Uncle Emmett on his deathbed that you'd Be A Writer Someday. Whatever your reasons for writing, you will be better positioned to plan the project, allocate the resources, sustain the effort, and enjoy the result if you understand those reasons.

So, why are you writing a business book? Only you can answer that question. And it is worth answering. An understanding of your motivations and goals should inform the whole publishing process, beginning with the development of the idea for the book.

Big Ideas

A book project requires three human elements: someone with an idea, someone who can write professionally, and someone with the credibility to land a book contract. Each type of writer—author, expert-author, and ghostwriter—contributes at least one of these elements to the project.

- Authors of their own books deliver all three elements. They have the idea for the book, the ability to write professionally, and the credibility to induce an editor to give them a book contract.
- Expert-authors have the idea and the credibility but lack the ability (or the time or patience) to write professionally.
- Ghostwriters can write professionally but they write books based on someone else's idea (typically an expert-author's). Sometimes a "ghostwriter" has an idea but needs an expert's credibility to land a book contract. In these cases, the two usually share credit as co-authors.

Where do business book authors get their ideas? More to the point, how can you find a new idea?

Here are half-a-dozen ways:
- Start with your business experience
- Repackage your existing material
- Use your strongest feelings
- Watch the business world
- Cross-pollinate
- Study the business book market

Start with Your Business Experience

Your experience is unique. Every consultant, entrepreneur, or executive has a unique way of working with a unique set of people with a unique set of needs. If your way of working doesn't seem unique to you, then you're not paying attention. You're not seeing the people involved and the particularity of their situations and your approach to them.

Richard Bolles was an unemployed Episcopal priest who started career counseling other men and women in his position. He began to write down his ideas, and that document evolved into *What Color Is Your Parachute?* Could another career counselor have written that book? No. But another career counselor could have written a book on its topic, which is how to find personally fulfilling work. Bolles' experience taught him that people stand a better chance of finding fulfilling work if they start by examining themselves and their needs rather than the job market and its needs.

What does your experience tell you about what works and what doesn't for you and for other people in business?

Repackage Your Existing Material

Many companies already have material—intellectual capital, if you will—that has been underutilized. This is often the case for training and consulting firms. If you have a seminar or workshop, or a proven process for accomplishing a complex task, you may well be able to structure it into a book. Bear in mind, though, that if you decide to develop a trade book, as opposed to a workbook, from this type of material, you can't just translate it into book form. You must use the coursework as a jumping-off point and rework it into a richly textured set of lessons clothed in anecdotes, examples, and cases. A reader of *Write to the Top* by Deborah Dumaine, president of Better Communications, Inc., would probably never suspect that some of the material in the book was drawn from the many corporate writing workshops the company had delivered before Dumaine decided to write the book. The product has to be that seamless (although you should certainly cite your background).

Service firms in businesses as diverse as software, water purification, design, health care, and risk management have developed books on the basis of what they do in the course of meeting their customers' needs. To be of real value to readers, these books must avoid self-serving ends and instead deliver solid, complete information in an engaging manner.

Original research undertaken either to support a book or for another purpose forms the basis of many business books. The academic rigor and the research and analytical skills of many consultants and most B-school professors provides the kind of rich raw material that publishers crave when times turn serious, as they currently have.

In other words, you can often find ideas and material for a book just by taking a good look around the office or at the work you have already done. But if the aim is to create a first-rate trade book, you must then extract the best ideas, build them up, and restructure, as well as repackage, the material for publication.

Follow Your Feelings

Emotion often demands expression. On the surface, Stephen Covey's *The Seven Habits of Highly Effective People* presents these habits. Yet the deeper message concerns something Covey feels quite strongly about: principle-centered management. Covey believes in managing your business and your life on the basis of sound moral principles. This belief fuels his book. Strong feelings also propel *In Search of Excellence*. In the December, 2001 issue of *Fast Company*, Tom Peters stated that he co-wrote the book partly because, "I was genuinely, deeply, sincerely, and passionately pissed off!" The object of his ire was command-and-control management.

In the early 1990s, managerial layoffs became routine and newspapers announced a "white-collar recession." I managed to survive several layoffs at a Fortune 500 company, yet I loathed the idea that my livelihood could be taken from me. That loathing compelled me to write a book called *Multipreneuring*, which urged managers and professionals to avoid dependence on one employer by developing multiple skills, careers, and income streams. The process of writing it prepared me to do the same.

Properly channeled, strong emotion drives creative thinking. It can also enliven an author's writing and drive her to finish the manuscript. If you feel strongly about something in the workplace, think about what would address those feelings, then write about it.

Watch the Business World

As the philosopher Yogi Berra said, "You can observe an awful lot just by watching." Where do you see unmet needs? What do your colleagues, customers, suppliers, and shareholders care most about? How do they operate?

Example: In an interview, a university president said that he pays close attention to complaints from the staff and students. He investigates complaints and, whenever possible, fixes whatever is causing them. He believes that the things people complain about, even petty annoyances, point to institutional inefficiencies and weaknesses. In contrast, most senior executives dismiss complaints as mere grousing from the troops. The university president's contrarian approach may constitute a new idea: To fix your organization, fix what people complain about. Could that be a book idea?

Cross-Pollinate

The idea-generating technique of cross-pollination, which consciously mixes concepts from two different disciplines, can be quite useful to authors. Actually, most idea-generating techniques, such as brainstorming and free association, work—if you use them. There's no need to cover these techniques here, but cross-pollination warrants mention because many business books apply concepts from other disciplines to business.

For instance, Margaret Wheatley's book *Management and the New Science* applies principles from quantum physics to business. Mark Bryan's book *The Artist's Way at Work* shows how to apply something of the artist's creativity to business. Books that adapt military strategies to business result from cross-pollination. So, in their way, do books that look to nonbusiness figures—everyone from Queen Elizabeth I to W.C. Fields—for business leadership lessons. In the cross-pollination race, John D. McDonald surely holds the winning trifecta ticket: He's the author of *Strategy in Poker, Business, and War*.

Which principles and practices from your life experience and general knowledge have applicability to business?

Study the Business Book Market

Finally, examine the market to ascertain what is and isn't being covered. Visit online bookstores like Amazon.com, bn.com, booksamillion.com, booksense.com, and 1800ceoread.com. Check out brick-and-mortar bookstores and notice how they classify and display business books. Leaf through the books, checking out tables of contents and snippets of text. Bookstores still give you the best feel for books. (Remember, despite the inroads that online bookstores have made and the value they've added, they account for only ten percent of all books sold.)

Examining the market might spark some ideas. It will also show how ideas for books in various subgenres—job search, leadership, investing, and so on—are packaged and positioned. Unfortunately, examining current titles will not tell you what editors are currently buying. It will tell you what they were buying twelve to twenty-four months ago. That's the average time between the purchase of a book proposal and the book's publication date.

Thus, a title in a bookstore resembles the light from a faraway star: The editor's desire for such a book may have flamed out before the title ever reached your gaze. This is one of several reasons to find an agent who regularly handles business books and who therefore knows what editors are buying.

This examination of the market should get you thinking about where in the market your book might fit, which is the major concern of an agent or editor considering a book idea.

How Agents and Editors Judge Book Ideas

Agents and editors apply four initial tests to a business book idea. These amount to subjective judgments about the quality of the idea, the audience for the book, the take-away value for the reader, and the promotability of the book.

Quality: A Good Idea

A good idea for a book must be rich enough to warrant about 60,000 words. There have been exceptions, including breakthrough books such as *The One Minute Manager*, but most business books reach the customary trade-book length. Therefore, one of the first questions editors ask themselves is, "Is this a book idea or an idea for a magazine article?" It's a test of the idea's richness.

A good idea snaps, crackles, and pops as it crosses the synapses. It generates material. It lends itself to quotes, anecdotes, war stories, and company case histories. It reminds people of situations they have faced and sparks other ideas. Some of these other ideas will be useful and many won't be. But it's a good sign if the idea leads to other ideas. If you pitch an idea and the catcher starts tossing out her own ideas, the idea is drawing a response and igniting people's thinking. Conversely, if you and everyone you talk to feel as if you're "pushing a string" rather than being pulled along by the idea, the idea may not be all that good.

There are ways to improve an idea, but the richer it is to begin with, the closer you are to a book deal.

Speaking of deals, a book idea that's good for one publisher may be useless to another. So first the editor must decide whether the idea fits the mission and current strategy of the publishing house. Some houses insist on substance and intellectual rigor, while others want flash and fun. Some stress how-to business books to the exclusion of narratives about companies or events, and some prefer more of a mix. At various times a house will alter its strategy to better capitalize on market trends. Again, an agent who handles business books will know which kinds of books each house is seeking.

Audience: The Bigger, the Better

Virtually any idea will interest some people, but trade-book publishers want ideas that will be of interest to tens of thousands, hundreds of thousands or, better yet, millions of people. So they reject ideas they see as too technical, too specialized, or targeted to too narrow an audience.

To motivate an agent or editor, a book idea should meet a clear, intense need in the marketplace. Buyers of how-to books want to make or save money, preferably the former. They hope to do this by improving their performance in some specific area: leading, selling, investing, communicating, hiring better employees, managing their careers or time or money more effectively, or enhancing their prestige or promotability.

The most salable ideas speak to basic wants. Most people want to be highly effective (*Seven Habits*). Most want fulfilling work (*Parachute*). And everyone wants to be rich (*Millionaire Next Door*). These sophisticated books speak to elemental needs.

Business books often tap two other basic drives: the need for security and the desire to stay informed. Some books blatantly appeal to people's fears. These include titles about protecting assets, coping with change, and profiting in the coming crash. Books on personal finance and retirement planning address the need for security. The desire to stay informed underlies purchases of books about business trends, fads, and new practices. Business trends include matters such as independent contracting (Daniel Pink's *Free Agent Nation*) and the speed of change (*Blur* by Christopher Meyer and Stan Davis) while practices can be as specific as properly staffing the organization (*Topgrading* by Bradford Smart) and making money with various technologies (*TechnoLeverage* by H. Michael Hruby).

Examine business book publishers' online or hard-copy catalogs and search online bookstores by publisher. You will notice that books from large houses, such as HarperBusiness and Wiley & Sons, typically target mass audiences while those from smaller houses, such as Career Press and Texere, often target narrower audiences. There's room in the business book market for large publishers seeking home runs and grand slams and for smaller outfits that do well on doubles, triples, and the occasional home run (and grand slam). But because every editor wants a best seller, an author should know how to target his book to the widest audience. Chapter 4 discusses ways of doing this in the book proposal.

Lessons Learned: Take-Away Value

Particularly with how-to and trend books, editors ask: What's the take-away value? A how-to book should give readers practical lessons, things they can do to make money, save money, or manage better. Books on trends should tell readers what action to take because of the trend. All advice must be practical and supported with examples. This all adds up to take-away value. The take-away value is the main selling point for the book, for both the publisher's sales force and the bookseller.

To develop take-away value, ask yourself: After reading this book, what should the reader do when he goes to work on Monday? Think about whether you will be able to demonstrate with real-world examples that your advice will work. Lack of real-life examples makes a book too theoretical—an instant turn-off—and often points to a lack of practical, take-away value.

Promotability: Hot, Hotter, Hottest

Ideally, a business book should be newsworthy, or at least promotable in print and broadcast media. The best book ideas are inherently promotable to a wide audience. They tap a widespread concern or some aspect of the zeitgeist. *Fast Food Nation*, Eric Schlosser's brilliant tour of the fast food industry, and *The Millionaire Next Door* by Ph.D.s Thomas J. Stanley and William D. Danko both key off of everyday concerns in dramatic ways. Hamburgers have phony flavoring from New Jersey? The guy mowing his lawn next door could be worth millions?

If your idea lacks that kind of ready-made promotability, realize that heat, like fame, can be generated on a small but still meaningful scale. For instance, business how-to will garner less news coverage than business exposé, but can still excite the people who care most about the subject. Today, specific periodicals, conferences, institutes, and associations focus on every aspect of business, including leadership, marketing, investing, strategy, diversity, and balancing home and family life. Learn who operates in these arenas, position the book to appeal to their interests, and to those people it will be very hot stuff.

In most cases the quality, audience, take-away value, and promotability of an idea can be increased through development.

Developing an Idea

Development makes an idea bigger, bolder, more appealing, more exciting. It does this by making it more specific, concrete, and easy to grasp and by raising the stakes for the reader. Development helps the agent and editor "see the book" in the proposal and moves the idea toward becoming a book.

Here's development in action: I worked with two successful businessmen, Tom Richardson and Augusto Vidaurreta, who had a system of managing business relationships with *all* stakeholders. They called their system Relationship Asset Management (RAM) and wanted to write a book by that name. The book would explain the system in the first two or three chapters and then have a chapter on each stakeholder group—employees, customers, suppliers, investors, competitors, banks, the media, the community, and so on.

The basic idea was excellent. While many books covered relationships with employees *or* customers *or* suppliers *or* investors, none considered every relationship with every stakeholder to be a valuable asset requiring active management. But the title Relationship Asset Management sounded technical and—because "asset management" is a financial term—a bit confusing. Also, devoting a chapter to each stakeholder, while logical, could create repetition by covering the same RAM principles for each group.

Development meant finding a new structure and title for the book. To solve the structural issue, we identified additional RAM principles and built the book around them rather than the stakeholder groups. The full title became *Business Is a Contact Sport: Using the 12 Principles of Relationship Asset Management to Build Buy-In, Blast Away Barriers, and Boost Your Business.* The proposal was sold to Alpha Books, who published the book nine months later. (You'll find a copy of this proposal in Appendix 1.)

Define the Idea in One Sentence

John D. Rockefeller, Sr., said, "If you can't write your idea on the back of your calling card, you don't have a clear idea." There are several ways to clarify a book idea, but essentially you must develop a short, crisp answer to the question: What is this book about? or What does this book do? The answer can be phrased in whatever way works best for you. One approach would be just to answer that question briefly and in your own words on paper. Another is to fill in the blanks in one or both of the following two statements.

> This book shows _____(your target readers) how to _____ (take-away value).

> or:

> When _____ (your target readers) read this book they will be able to _____ (the skill they will learn).

For instance:

> This book shows <u>people at all levels, in and out of business</u> how to <u>use a stress-free, five-step program for getting more done</u>.

> When <u>senior executives</u> read this book they will be able to <u>create a culture in which people hold themselves accountable for getting results</u>.

The first statement sums up David Allen's book *Getting Things Done*, while the second sums up *Journey to the Emerald City* by Roger Connors and Tom Smith. Two different books with very different types of titles and messages, but both summarized in one sentence.

To create clarity, be as specific as possible in filling in the blanks. New authors often worry that being specific will shut out some readers or some aspects of the topic. They assume that's bad. Actually, it's good. Although editors want big ideas for large audiences, they want sharply focused ideas, not cosmic concepts or vague notions. A clear idea, expressed concisely, becomes the North Star for the author, agent, and everyone else on the project. That North Star soon leads the author to the ideal title and positioning strategy for the book.

Titles and Positioning

The title and subtitle position the idea in people's minds and ultimately position the book in the marketplace. Even a very basic title can position a book in an interesting way. For instance, the title *Getting Things Done* is utterly straightforward. The book has a great subtitle—*The Art of Stress-Free Productivity*—which adds value but isn't really necessary. *Getting Things Done* is a book about getting organized. But it is *not positioned* as a book about getting organized. It is positioned as a book on personal productivity. What's more exciting—getting organized or boosting your productivity? The book covers organizing paper flows, setting up files, prioritizing tasks, and other essentials of being organized. Yet the title sells none of this. Instead, it sells the sizzle, makes a promise, and summarizes the take-away value: Read this book and you'll get things done.

The Twenty-Second Sell

Publishers say that a salesperson has about 20 seconds to sell a book to a bookseller. To free up time for those hard-working salespeople and to help your agent get you a book contract, try to get the pitch down to ten seconds or less. The ideas for most breakthrough books are easily summarized:

- *The One Minute Manager.* If you know what you're doing, it takes only a minute to be a good manager in a given situation.
- *The Change Monster.* Managing change is monstrous, but monsters can usually be killed.
- *The Seven Habits of Highly Effective People.* Do these seven things consistently and you will become successful in all areas of life.
- *The Mind of the CEO.* When you look inside the minds of CEOs and see how they think, you can think the way they do and be as successful.
- *In Search of Excellence.* We looked at what makes companies successful, and you'll learn what those things are in this book.
- *Guerrilla Marketing.* You don't need a big budget or massive resources to market your product or service effectively.
- *The Millionaire Next Door.* Your neighbor who owns the lumber yard may be wealthier than the bond traders downtown, and you can learn how he got that way.

The common theme in all these books, and in most how-to business books, boils down to Secrets of Success. The author knows something, has learned something, or has developed something that will help readers become more successful in some area. The book will show readers what that something is and how to use it.

Go for the Title

Once you have defined and refined the idea, you must develop a working title. This may seem premature at this stage, and for some authors it may be. However, a title sharpens your thinking about the idea and helps the book gel. Even a working title that will change several times during development lends shape to a book. The right title can also ignite the writing process. For instance, the title *Business Is a Contact Sport* prompted us to use quotes and concepts from the world of sports in the proposal.

Developing a title is a creative endeavor, which means more brainstorming, free-associating, and cross-pollinating—then refining the results. Open up your thinking. Turn to the dictionary and the thesaurus. Flip through magazines. Collaborate. Kick ideas around. Solicit reactions. Forget the whole thing for a day or two and then come back to it. And consider these guidelines:

1. Try for a title that sums up a benefit for the reader in colloquial terms. Good examples include *Starting on a Shoestring*, *Go Hire Yourself an Employer*, and *Swim with the Sharks without Being Eaten Alive*.

2. Use a title that people with a high school education could readily grasp, even if the book targets MBAs. Avoid big words and vague concepts (a lesson I learned from using the title *Multipreneuring*.) It is easy to get too fancy. The more vivid the picture a title paints, the better.

3. Although they go against the notion that clarity sells, business books with "mystery titles" can catch on. *What Color Is Your Parachute?* has nothing to do with skydiving, and *The Fifth Discipline* doesn't even hint at what the first four disciplines might be. But both books are business classics.

4. Use a subtitle in almost all cases. It's a convention, but a worthwhile one because it usually clarifies the book's subject. If the book doesn't need a subtitle, go ahead and skip it. But most business books benefit from one.

5. If the book targets a very specific audience, try to reach that

audience through the title. *Things Mother Never Taught You*, *Why Should White Guys Have All the Fun?* and *Get a Financial Life* target, respectively, the female, African-American, and young adult markets.

6. Slang terms and common expressions often work well. The terms bulletproof and guerrilla—as in *Bulletproof Your Resume* and *Guerrilla Marketing*—worked so well that they each led to a series. Buzzwords or popular tag lines can work, but the title might age quickly. Even so, *Breaking the Glass Ceiling* holds up because the metaphor is (unfortunately) durable.

7. Speaking of metaphors, handle them with care. A metaphor running amok can trample the material and annoy the reader. At the moment, "metaphor titles" are out of vogue with editors. If you do use a metaphor title, pick a flexible, durable one and weave it *lightly* into the book (as Connors and Smith did in *Journey to the Emerald City*).

8. Finally, check *Books In Print* and online bookstores to make sure the title isn't taken. Titles cannot be copyrighted (although they can be trademarked) but it is unprofessional, unoriginal, and confusing to steal a title from another book.

Titles can change in the publishing process. The publisher's sales people may hate a title, or it may sound too much like another title, or it may be too long or too short or too vague or too vulgar. Don't consider a title final until it's on the dust jacket.

Testing, Testing

It's easy to fall in love with an idea or a title and wind up broken-hearted when things don't work out. Before you get too involved, test the idea and title with a few people, including a few who work outside of business. Although you may believe the idea represents a total breakthrough, in fact few business book topics with broad or even niche audiences have not been repeatedly covered, and many titles have already been used in one form or another.

Online bookstores supply the fastest way to test an idea for its originality. Simply go to the search function, input the key subject word or words—leadership or leading change, job interviews or resume writing—and stand back. Scores, often hundreds, of titles will pop up. Even a search on your title or on key words from your title may locate a book or two.

If you see that your book has been "done before," don't despair. Instead try to differentiate and reposition it. Evergreen topics stay green because authors develop new ways of looking at them and presenting them. You may be able to tweak, twist, or recast the idea for a new audience. To take an example, personal finance books had been done to death. But *Get a Financial Life* by Beth Kobliner sold well because it was a personal finance book for people in their twenties and thirties.

If your title has been taken or close to taken, your task is merely to develop a new one, which is easier than reworking the idea itself. This calls for heavy brainstorming, cross-pollination, and exercises in word play and imagery. If all else fails, plug in a plain vanilla title for now, something like *21st Century Quality Control* or *Making Money in Real Estate*, and revisit the whole issue later, after you have further elaborated the idea.

The second way to test an idea or a title is to present it, preferably on paper, to several people whose opinions you value. Run the idea or the title and subtitle past one person at a time, rather than a group, where people often sway one another's responses. (Besides, people don't shop for books in groups.) People should be able to "get" the idea of the book from the title and subtitle. If they get it from the title alone, so much the better. Ask why your respondents like or dislike a title. Be careful if your respondents find a title "cute." Cute can work, or it can work against you. If you like a "cute" title, listen carefully to the opinions of those who don't. Finally, people should find the title memorable. A forgettable title does nothing for a book.

I generally test two or three titles at a time with several people individually to see which works best. The results often surprise me and change my mind about a title I thought was a sure winner.

Where the Idea Is Going

The idea forms the core of the book's content. The title is the label on the package. The content and its package are presented to agents and editors in a book proposal, a document covered in detail in Chapters 4 and 5. But before we start writing the proposal, let's examine the path to a book contract. Traveling this path entails finding an agent to represent the book proposal and, with the help of that agent, finding an editor who wants to publish the proposed book badly enough to offer you a book contract and an advance.

3

The Fast Track to a Book Deal

Getting an Agent and Landing a Business Book Contract

In a trade book deal, an editor offers the author a royalty on future sales of the book, an advance against those royalties (usually), and a commitment to publish the proposed book. This chapter examines the business side of getting a business book deal. Chapters 4 and 5 cover the writing side of getting a deal—developing the book proposal.

Having the right agent will do more to compress the time it takes you to get a book deal than any other single factor. So, the fast-track to a business book deal involves two phases: Phase I, which is finding the right agent, and Phase II, which is finding the right publisher, with the help of that agent. Each phase comprises several steps.

Phase I: Getting an Agent

Many first-time authors believe they don't need an agent, which is a shame because they are the authors who need one the most. An agent acts as the front-line critic of a book proposal. Publishers that don't accept unagented proposals—and even those that do—value the "filtering" function agents perform. Unfortunately, when an agent declines to represent a proposal, she usually offers the author little, if any, constructive criticism. On the other hand, an agent who does want to represent a proposal usually has a few ideas for making it more marketable. These ideas are worth hearing. Moreover, a good agent can get an editor excited about a proposal, and move it on to a faster track for consideration.

An agent can typically get a larger advance for a given proposal than its author. So it's false economy to try to save the agent's fifteen percent commission (on the advance and royalties). If an author sells a proposal for an advance of $15,000, he saves $2,250 ($= \$15,000 \times 15\%$). He keeps one hundred percent of $15,000. If an agent can get a mere $5,000 more, the author keeps eighty-five percent of $20,000 or $17,000 ($= \$20,000 \times 85\%$). If the agent can get, say, $30,000, the author keeps $25,500. And so on.

Agents draw forth higher advances because they know which editors want which material and what they will pay for it. Editors aim to buy promising books for the lowest price acceptable to the author. Agents have a loftier view of "acceptable" than many authors. Hard-bargaining agents make editors pay for books they want to publish. It is true that not all agents bargain hard. It is also true that not all authors write books that sell well. In those cases, an agent can bring authors' expectations more in line with the economic realities of book publishing.

Finally, an agent who will spend time coaching his authors before their books start to sell will teach them a lot about publishing. Agents can interpret the often mysterious moves of a publishing house and even lobby against decisions that could harm the book, such as a badly designed cover or an unfavorable publication date.

On a net basis, a good agent repays the time and effort it takes to find one and definitely earns his piece of the action.

How to Land an Agent

Many literary agents don't represent business books, represent very few, or deal only with celebrity-CEOs. Few specialize in the genre and those that do also represent other material, usually self-help books and other popular nonfiction. A business book need not be represented by an agent who specializes in them. However, it should be represented by an agent who knows the genre and has relationships with editors who publish them. (A good number of editors handle only business books.)

Barring the lucky introduction, the process of finding a literary agent who handles business books breaks down as follows:

1. Research business book agents
2. Research business book publishers and editors
3. Approach the agents and submit the material
4. Sign with an agent

Research Business Book Agents

Several good reference sources list literary agents, including *Literary Market Place*, published by R. R. Bowker, *Guide to Literary Agents*, published by Writer's Digest Books, and *Writer's Guide to Book Editors, Publishers, and Literary Agents* by Jeff Herman, published by Prima Publishing. Each of these books has its advantages and each of them has enthusiastic fans among professional authors. At least one belongs on the bookshelf of every working writer.

Literary Market Place, or LPM in the vernacular, is the gold standard of publishing industry reference books. It is the broadest compendium of the various players in book publishing, including publishers, agents, publicity firms, distributors, and suppliers. At $299 in hard copy, it's also the most expensive. Happily, the Web-based version (www.literarymarketplace.com) provides even greater functionality at a lower price.

The Writer's Digest *Guide to Literary Agents* provides detailed listings on over five hundred agents, most of whom focus exclusively on trade books. Information includes the agency's address and phone number, names of individual agents, openness to new authors, types of books handled, recent titles sold, and query guidelines. (Pay particular attention to that last item.) This book is probably the best source of information on which agents handle business books, because it provides detailed information on the genres of books the agency represents—and it's cross-indexed by genre represented.

The *Writer's Guide to Book Editors, Publishers, and Literary Agents* lists publishers and editors, as well as agents, and comes in both CD-ROM and softcover versions. With only two hundred or so agent listings (as opposed to more than five hundred in the Writer's Digest *Guide*), it's not as exhaustive in its coverage. But Jeff Herman, who is an agent himself, also provides personal information on our quarry, such as university attended, and the agents' comments on everything from why they became agents to their quite revealing thoughts on their "client from hell."

Each of these books is extremely useful in its way. *Literary Market Place* and Jeff Herman's *Writers' Guide* provide one-volume overviews of the business that go beyond the Writer's Digest *Guide*, which covers only literary agents. (The Writer's Digest single-volume guide to the industry is *Writer's Market*, which is published annually and lists hundreds of book publishers and thousands of periodicals, but only seventy-five agents. *Writer's Market* also comes in a CD-ROM version and an on-line version at www.writersmarket.com.) Both the Writer's Digest *Guide to Literary Agents* and the *Writer's Guide to Book Editors, Publishers, and Literary Agents* include articles on topics such as how to make proper submissions to agents and what to expect from the author-agent relationship.

Aside from literarymarketplace.com and writersmarket.com, the Web *currently* remains less useful for this kind of research. The major professional organization for literary agents, the New York-based Association of Authors' Representatives, does maintain a site (www.aar-online.org) worth visiting. It includes a list of the 250 member agencies, the AAR Code of Ethics, and good questions to ask an agent, but it provides little information on what kind of material the listed agents handle. Besides, many good literary agents are not AAR members. Two other online sources are literaryagent.com and the Web sites of the agencies themselves, if they have one (unfortunately, many do not). The Web changes daily, so it wouldn't hurt to go back and check out these sites occasionally or run a Web search to see whether anything new turns up.

Another good way to find an agent is by checking the acknowledgments page of a business book you've liked. Many acknowledgments pages include a tip-of-the-hat to the agent on the project. The agency isn't usually mentioned, but that's not a problem. When you find an agent named in a book you like, simply refer to the agent index in one of the sources mentioned above for his agency and its location.

Look for agents who represent business, management, personal finance, and investment books. At last count, the Writer's Digest *Guide to Literary Agents* listed more than thirty agencies fitting this profile. Don't worry too much about geography. Location is less important than it was in the days when almost all literary agents were based in New York City. Many good agents now operate west of the Hudson River.

After research, it's time to target. Targeting means winnowing your list down to the five or six agents you think could best represent your book proposal. Have a second list of an additional five or six agents in case the first batch doesn't pan out, and a third batch just to be safe.

It might seem smart to approach your second or third choices first, for practice. If you follow the advice in this and other books on the subject, that shouldn't be necessary. Furthermore, if a second-choice agent agrees to represent the project and you turn her down and then fail to find another agent, approaching her again would be awkward, to put it mildly. Better to target agents carefully and approach them seriously.

Research Business Book Publishers and Editors

Why research publishers when an agent will be presenting the proposal to them? Because you'll understand more of what your agent says if you know who publishes business books.

Again, *Literary Market Place* and *Writer's Guide to Book Editors, Publishers, and Literary Agents* are excellent sources, as is *Writer's Market*, published annually by Writer's Digest Books. To save you some work, Appendix 2 lists business book publishers and imprints but not editors, because editorial turnover is too high. Checking out their Web sites can tell you a lot about the books they publish and their approach to the market. Again, check the acknowledgments pages of business books for editors. If some of them are no longer with the same publishers, the sources I've mentioned (which are updated annually) might reveal their current whereabouts.

The amount of research you do on publishers depends on your level of interest. You could forgo this research entirely and depend on your agent's contacts. However, being knowledgeable always helps. Your research may also unearth publishers you think might be interested in your proposal. If so, mention them after you sign with an agent and listen to his opinion of them.

Sample Query Letter

Dear Ms. Jones:

Many successful books have focused on the small-office/home-office market. These include *How to Grow a Business* and *The Complete Idiot's Guide to Starting Your Own Business* (one of the best-selling business books in the *Idiot's* series). However, few books have shown readers how to grow a small business into a large one.

I have written a proposal for a business trade book called *The Million Dollar Mark: Sixteen Breakthrough Strategies for Your Small Business*. This book of sixteen chapters focuses on sixteen small businesses with over $1 million in annual sales—and reveals how they reached that level.

I've identified the businesses, and they have agreed to share their stories openly. In case some drop out of the project, I've identified another twelve likely participants who would work well in the book. Although this is my first book, I have written freelance articles for *Boston Business Journal* and the *Los Angeles Times* (business section).

I am seeking representation for the project and would greatly appreciate your reviewing the proposal and considering it for representation. Thank you for your time and consideration.

Sincerely,

John Q. Author

Approach Business Book Agents

Virtually all literary agents prefer query letters to phone calls, which they discourage from people they don't know. Most agents also prefer that authors they don't know send a query letter rather than a full proposal. (Agents will often review unsolicited proposals, but it's more economical to send a query letter first. You'll also get a faster reply.) The query letter describes the book, its market, the need it fills, and the author's qualifications—in one page, if at all possible. If she's interested, the agent will call or write to request the proposal. If she's not interested, you will almost always receive a rejection letter.

The sample query letter on the previous page is baloney-free because the writer has the goods. He has a solid idea, has compared the book to other successful ones, has properly set up the project (the back-up participants are a nice touch), and has some business writing experience. No amount of clever or ingratiating prose can mask the absence of these things.

A good query letter mailed to a well-researched list of five or six agents should motivate at least one to request the proposal. If more than one agent requests the proposal, protocol dictates that you should inform them that other agents are also reviewing it. Some agents state in their submission guidelines that they do not accept simultaneous submissions. They don't want to spend time reviewing a proposal that might be pulled from them. (All agents read simultaneous query letters.)

You usually get one shot at an agent on a given project, so make it count. Agents readily recognize amateurish material, so submit only your best work. In other words, have a well-written proposal that you deeply believe in ready for the agent to review. It's not necessary to have a proposal of the length and depth described in Chapters 4 and 5 and shown in Appendix 1. But the agent will want a title, a table of contents, and at least several pages describing the book, competitive books, and the author's qualifications. She can probably decide whether she's interested based on this material, but she will need a full proposal to get a novice author a deal with a substantial publisher. In my view, authors with a well-written, full-length, ready-to-go proposal stand the best chance of getting on a fast track with an agent.

Signing with an Agent

When an agent calls and expresses interest or agrees to represent the book, before you consummate the relationship have an in-depth conversation so you can learn more about one another. Agents dislike "auditioning" for authors, but some questions are certainly in order, including:

- What attracts you to the material? How could it be improved?
- In general, how do you prefer to communicate with your authors—phone, mail, e-mail?
- Do you use a written contract? Can you fax me a copy of it?
- What is your fee? Do you charge expenses, such as photo-copying and postage, back to authors? (If she is sending a copy of the contract, it will note the fees and expenses, so you need not ask these questions.)
- How long have you been at this agency? How long have you been an agent? What were you doing before?
- Can you tell me about a few business titles you represented? Which publishers did you place them with?
- Can you give me the name of another business book author you represent so I can get that person's perspective on your agency? (She may not like "providing a reference," but it shouldn't hurt to ask.)

Be prepared to answer questions about your ambitions as an author and plans to achieve them (without sounding wide-eyed or long-winded). If nothing disastrous occurs, the two of you will probably move to the next phase. Depending on geography, you may or may not be able to meet in person before agreeing on representation. While a lot of publishing business goes on between parties who have never met in person, writers should meet their agents face-to-face if possible. It adds a personal dimension and builds trust in ways that the telephone and e-mail cannot.

Detailed coverage of the author-agent relationship is beyond the scope of this book. Agency contracts, services performed, and operating practices vary widely. However, Appendix 2 lists several sources for in-depth information on landing an agent and managing the author-agent relationship. Just keep in mind that the right agent will get you a book deal faster than any other single factor.

Phase II: Finding a Publisher

With a book proposal in hand, the hunt for a publisher begins. This section addresses finding a publisher either with or without an agent. In either case, the major tasks are twofold: approaching the editors and submitting material, and negotiating the book contract.

Approaching Editors Through an Agent

An agent regularly talks with editors about their wants and needs. Therefore, she is positioned to pitch your book idea to editors she judges to be receptive. The agent will send the proposal to those who express interest in it. This does not, however, relegate you to the role of bystander.

To support your agent and stay on the fast track you must:

- Supply your agent with the number of copies of the proposal she specifies, in perfect condition
- Understand the agent's sales strategy and way of working—the publishers she intends to approach, expected timeframe for rejections and offers, and frequency of her updates to you. Setting expectations explicitly at the outset saves wear and tear on both parties.
- Trust the agent to do her job, and let the process take its course. If you hear or read something the agent should

know about, pass it on to her. But curb any urge to badger her or to call for constant updates.

- Respond quickly to any request from editors, which will usually come through the agent. They often want more information on an author's background, research for the book, or promotion plan. Update your agent promptly on *any* contact you have with an editor regarding the project.
- Discuss only editorial and creative issues with an editor who gets in touch with you. Refer the editor to your agent on any question related to the advance, royalty rate, hardcover versus softcover, or any other financial or business issue.

Your agent should return your calls, share information, and exhibit optimism about the project and its prospects. If any of these is absent, discuss the issue. That said, please realize that it's easy to think that your agent is dragging her feet, being unresponsive, losing enthusiasm, or conspiring with editors against you. For reasons yet to be fathomed, writing books and dealing with publishers generates a fair degree of paranoia in authors. Allow for this, and don't become alarmed if about two months go by with no displays of editorial interest.

If there's no offer in the works after a couple of months or so, it's time to assess the situation. How many rejections have you received, and from whom? What do accompanying comments tell you, if anything? Set aside time with your agent to discuss possible changes in strategy. These might include revamping the proposal, attaching other elements to the proposal (such as an association's brand or a foreword by a high-profile executive), or targeting smaller or more specialized publishers.

Eventually, most commercially viable material does find a home. Sit tight and keep the faith.

Approaching Editors Without an Agent

If you have decided to sell your proposal directly to a publisher, write query letters—modeled on the one provided for agents above—to editors you have identified as likely prospects. Approach only two or three at a time so you can modify the query letter or proposal as you go through the learning process. Also, be sure to enclose a self-addressed stamped envelope, and:

- When an editor requests the proposal, send one promptly. (Unless overnight delivery is requested, priority mail will do). If it's under review elsewhere, mention it if asked but be appropriately vague.

- Don't badger the editor, but do follow up in about four weeks and then every two or three weeks thereafter.

- Try to gauge the level of interest in the proposal. If there is some, ask if the editor plans to present it at an editorial meeting. If he does, ask when that meeting will occur because you would "like to get a sense of the timeframe." Then follow up a few days after that date.

- If the editor lacks interest or doesn't feel the proposal is fit to present at an editorial meeting, try to find out why. Ask what might make the proposal more attractive. If they have a similar book in process or they just dislike the idea, the proposal is dead at that house. But if the editor is on the fence, there may be something in the approach or structure of the book or in the author's platform that can be addressed.

- Stay focused on getting an offer. Avoid making statements that move you away from an offer and try to address any negatives that the editor raises, for instance about the size of the target market or the poor sales of competing books. Keep the discussion focused on how the book will find its market and why it will sell.

- If you strike out a few times or feel out of your depth, reconsider the decision to forgo an agent. Selling is difficult, and representing literary material is a particularly difficult form of selling.

Negotiate the Book Contract

With luck, sooner or later an editor will make an offer. When that happens, you are close to having a book contract. But you don't have one yet, nor do you have any guarantee of a good contract. It is easy for an author, particularly a new author or an author with only one idea, to be taken to the cleaners. Editors know that authors want to see themselves in print. They also negotiate book contracts every day. So beware—even if you have an agent. Agents often overlook things that come back to haunt an author months or even years after she signs the contract. It shouldn't happen, but it does.

What Is an Offer?

An offer is not a book contract. Rather it is an offer to extend a book contract. The sequence goes like this: On the basis of the proposal, the publisher offers the author an advance which (theoretically) finances the writing of the manuscript. The offer is conveyed from the editor to the author through the author's agent, if he has one. The offer is subject to negotiation. As noted, some agents bargain harder than others. Some counter the editor's offer even before conveying it to the author. Others tell the author about the offer and then strategize about whether to accept, counter, or refuse it. When the author accepts the offer, the publisher's legal department produces a contract, which the author and the publisher (but not the agent) will sign.

Negotiating deals stands outside the scope of this book. However, the following words of advice, learned the hard way, may help you get a better deal:

Never agree to "an offer," no matter what an agent or editor says, without knowing five things:
1. amount of the advance
2. payout schedule of the advance
3. royalty rates, escalation points, and the value to which the royalty rates are applied
4. format of the book (hardcover or softcover)
5. delivery date of the manuscript

Although many "offers" mention only the advance, and perhaps one or two of the other items, all five are important. They should all be part of the offer and should be settled before the book contract is drawn up.

The *amount of the advance* is the amount that the publisher will pay you for writing and delivering the manuscript. It is an advance against royalties and other proceeds from the book, such as film rights. For how-to business books (which are not exactly hot properties in Hollywood) the most significant other proceeds come from foreign rights sales. The author receives no money beyond the advance until the book earns out the advance.

Long-standing questions about advances abound. Does a large one commit the publisher to spending more on publicity? Not always. Does a small advance doom a book to failure? Again, not always. If a book with a large advance doesn't earn out, do other publishers count it against the author? Maybe, maybe not. In general, however, as in other business situations, the more money you receive, the better.

The standard *payout schedule of the advance* is one-third on signing the contract, one-third on delivery of the first half of the manuscript, and one-third on delivery and editorial acceptance of the entire manuscript (meaning that it is accepted as publishable). Another common arrangement is one-half on signing and one-half on acceptance of the manuscript, although the manuscript may still be delivered in thirds.

Some contracts pay the author the final third of the advance three or six months *after* acceptance of the manuscript. Worse yet, some tie the final payment to the *publication date*. This places the author's final payment at risk. What if the publisher decides not to publish the book? (It's rare, but it happens.) Moreover, is it really an "advance" if the book is being sold to the public before the author gets his final payment? Insist on a reasonable payout schedule and avoid having payments tied to the publication date, which you don't control.

The standard hardcover *royalty rates* and *escalation points* are 10 percent on the first 5,000 copies of the book sold (not counting sales to book clubs and to the author), 12.5 percent on the next 5,000 copies, and 15 percent on all copies thereafter. Softcover rates vary more, but 6 percent on the first 10,000 copies sold and at least 7.5 percent on sales over that amount would be a reasonable minimum.

These "standard" rates have traditionally been applied to the retail price of the book. Yet many contracts now apply them to the net price, that is, the price that the publisher receives for the books, which is about fifty percent of the cover price. This amounts to a halving of the royalty rate. In other words, you get what you negotiate.

The *format of the book* should usually be hardcover. Although some authors believe that a book will sell more copies in softcover, it's not necessarily true. Hardcover books command more attention from reviewers, journalists, and the media in general. For an expert-author, hardcover means more prestige. Softcover is wonderful for subsequent editions of books initially released in hardcover, for some books on job hunting and other basic business skills, and for series such as *Dummies* and *Idiot's* guides. But in general, shoot for publication in hardcover. It shows more commitment to the book on the publisher's part, since hardcover books are a bit more expensive to manufacture. In any event, there's no reason a publisher can't decide on the format when making an offer. An author I know signed a so-called hard-soft deal, which let the publisher decide the format upon publication. The acquiring editor left the house and the publisher chose a softcover release, over the author's objections.

The *delivery date of the manuscript* must often be negotiated. As noted in the next chapter, the proposal contains a proposed delivery date, expressed as a season, for instance, spring 2006. If the proposal contains a completed introduction and sample chapter— and the editor wants to publish them as is—allow nine months to a year to write the book. This reflects a realistic estimate and should jibe with publisher's schedule. If the book needs a new introduction and first chapter, or intensive research, allow twelve to fifteen or even eighteen months.

Editors often want short deadlines for business books, nine or even six months, even when a short deadline might undermine the book's quality. The editor may know of a competitive book in the works at another house, or she may be trying to get the market timing just right. Try to negotiate the time you need to write the book well, but think hard before letting a deadline kill a deal. As Chapter 7 explains, there are ways of dealing with short deadlines.

Nail down these five specific items *before going to contract*, when the editor extends an offer. Once you accept the offer, you have much less room for negotiating these important terms.

Index Fun

Although less is riding on whether the book will have an index, it's good to have early agreement on the issue. Trade business books benefit from an index. It creates a more professional and finished look and allows browsers to search for entries that interest them. Even if they don't find exactly what they were looking for, they'll often come across something they like.

Make sure the contract stipulates that the book will have an index. Most publishers routinely include them in their books, and thus in their contracts, but not all do so for every book. There is also the matter of who pays for the index. The publisher should pay for the compilation of the index, a task usually performed by a freelance. However, some publishers pass the expense on to the author by deducting it from royalties.

If the editor balks at including an index by contractual agreement, offer to have the fee charged against the advance or royalties. That may shame the publisher into paying for it. At a minimum, the publisher should hire the freelance and pass the expense through to you. If that fails, you will need to hire an indexer or compile the index yourself, as long as the publisher is willing to pay for the few extra pages in each book.

Multiple Offers

Agents have their ways of handling (and creating) situations in which more than one publisher extends an offer on a book. How and whether this happens depends upon your agent's clout with editors and on the interest your book generates among them. Very rarely, an agent may be able to hold an auction, which means that she distributes the proposal to editors, sets a deadline for offers, and you accept the most attractive one.

Try to understand your agent's thought process as you discuss multiple offers. The most attractive offer may not always be the one with the highest advance. As I have said, there are other factors to consider, including the payout schedule and royalty rates, as well as something more intangible—the editor's enthusiasm for the book. This can be important. If an editor connects with the material or sees the book as a career-maker (for herself, that is), she may push the production, marketing, publicity, and sales people in ways that she would not if that enthusiasm were absent.

Going to Contract

Whoever draws up a contract does so to enhance their own interests, and publishers are no exception. If you've settled the issues we've discussed so far, you have a good offer and a solid level of commitment from the publisher. You or, better yet, your agent should raise the few really important contract provisions after you've accepted the offer and before you go to contract. In my experience, these are usually discussed after the author and agent have the contract in hand, which places them in the position of "asking for changes" rather than truly negotiating.

Negotiating the terms of the contract (as opposed to the offer) can be difficult for several reasons. Editors can become irritated with authors who present a laundry list of items needing alteration in the contract and clauses of their own to insert. It's not in your interest to be labeled a pain, particularly early in the publishing process, over something relatively unimportant. Moreover, established publishers have worked out their standard contracts over time. They are not about to ignore the evidence of their experience and the advice of their attorneys. If you're a celebrity-CEO or have sold hundreds of thousands of books, you have leverage. However, most houses depart very little from their standard contract.

Essentially, the publisher wants to ensure that your manuscript will be original, free of libel and plagiarism, and acceptable for publication. That last item is a subjective judgment, but one that's almost always fairly rendered. The publisher also wants the manuscript delivered on time. These are all reasonable requirements.

In contract negotiations, focus on the few things that you really want. I am not an attorney, nor am I dispensing legal advice. But from my viewpoint as an author, there are four items in book contracts of particular importance to both working writers and expert-authors of business books:

- publisher's rights to your work
- author's copies and author's discount
- publisher's stake in your next book
- publisher's promotional resources

Publisher's Rights to Your Work

The publisher is buying the right to publish the manuscript and a stake in properties derived directly from the manuscript. The properties involved include the hardcover edition, softcover edition, subsequent editions, foreign language editions, audiobooks, film and television rights, and electronic rights.

As a practical matter, you must ensure two things: First, you must retain the right to create seminars, white papers, and other forms of expression of the ideas in the book. This right is not abridged by the book contracts I have seen and signed. Second, rights that the publisher retains but does not make use of should revert to you at some point, for example, in two years. Few standard contracts explicitly state that rights revert to the author if not exercised.

This can be an important issue. Suppose that in two years you want to produce an audiobook or publish a CD-ROM version of the book. Suppose further that you believe you can turn a profit on these products even if only a few thousand are sold. That profit may be meaningful to you but not to the publisher. If you don't have these rights, you'll need the publisher's permission to produce these products. They may say yes. They may say no. They may say, yes if we get twenty-five percent of the sales revenue as a royalty. It all depends on how they feel at the time *unless* the rights revert to you in full at some point in the future. Also, whenever a book of yours goes out of print, immediately request in writing that all rights revert to you unless you already have them.

Author's Copies and Author's Discount
These items are particularly important for authors who need books to market their companies.

Most publishing contracts state that the author will be sent a number of free copies upon publication. That number usually ranges from ten to forty. Push for as many copies as your agent believes you can reasonably request. If you don't have an agent, ask for one hundred copies and see what you can get. Also, try to get the deepest possible discount off the cover price for copies that you will be buying.

Why? Well, first, giving away copies of a book generates sales. Word-of-mouth, a powerful marketing tool, comes about when people read the book and recommend it to others. In addition, if the book is to serve as a business development tool for a consultant, company, or product line, then the cost of the books can add up. So it's in an author's interest to get the best price from the publisher on his own books.

Book contracts usually state that the publisher will sell copies of the book to the author at the "author's discount" of fifty percent off the cover price. This is not exactly a bargain. Retailers (who didn't write the book) get the same discount. Try to negotiate a deeper discount, particularly if you need books as calling cards for your business. One author I know of got sixty-five percent off. As I noted earlier, copies of the book purchased by the author generate no royalties.

Publisher's Stake in Your Next Book
If your book is successful, the publisher will want first crack at your next book. That's reasonable, given that they played a role in

that success. They may even offer a two-book deal: a contract for the book you've proposed and for your next book as well. Multi-book contracts are rare, however, except for established authors. Still, most book contracts do give the publisher first look at the author's next book.

Most contracts also contain language that limits your ability to publish another book on a similar topic until the book under contract has been published. This too is reasonable. Publishers shouldn't have to compete against the author when they publish his work.

Watch out though: First-look and noncompete clauses sometimes contain language that can tie up an author's next book for quite a while. An author or ghostwriter who plans to write another book must review that language carefully. An author I know wrote a business book with a colleague of his and signed a contract that prohibited him from even proposing a book to another publisher—with or without that collaborator—until *after the publication date* of the book under contract. The publisher also got first-look at that next proposal and 45 days to acquire it or reject it. The publisher exercised this right, tying up a proposal this author wrote for a book on an unrelated topic with another colleague for more than a year.

As with the issue of advances, any restrictive clauses that involve the publication date of the book under contract are dangerous because the publisher controls that date. If the publisher pushes the book back an entire season, or two, that may be an excellent business decision. But it could leave your next book or your final payment hanging.

People who write books for a living cannot afford to have their ability to pitch proposals and get books published curtailed by legal language. Of course, it's an agent's job to have language like that removed or modified. But some agents don't read every clause in their authors' contracts, and others don't negotiate vigorously. Because you must live with the contract, you must—without alienating anyone—ensure that the contract is as fair to you as it is to the publisher. Try to conduct all contract negotiations through your agent. This keeps the relationship between you and your editor focused on creative issues. Listen to your agent and heed his guidance, but be sure you understand the trade-offs and potential downside in any agreement you sign.

There are several excellent sources of information for generalists on the legal aspects of book contracts. *Kirsch's Guide to the Book Contract* by Los Angeles-based publishing attorney Jonathan Kirsch breaks down the book contract into understandable terms by use of a model contract and plain English. *How to Be Your Own Literary Agent: The Business of Getting Published* by literary agent Richard Curtis is, as the subtitle indicates, a primer on book publishing and covers negotiating book contracts particularly well. Just take the first couple of chapters, in which Curtis paints a bleak picture of new authors' chances of seeing publication, with a grain of salt. New authors (even new authors without agents) are always breaking into print. Finally, the Author's Guild and other writers' organizations provide their members with useful guides to book contracts, as well as work-for-hire agreements and other contracts that writers encounter.

It can take weeks, even months, for the contract to emerge from the legal department of a publishing house. Make sure that your agent and editor know that you do not view the contract as a mere formality and that you need to see it ASAP. The inordinate amount of time that many publishers take to issue their "standard contract" is another mystery of the publishing business. It's also one more reason to nail down the key provisions of your deal *before* agreeing to the offer and going to contract.

Publisher's Promotional Resources

New authors are often under the impression that publishers mount book tours and publicity campaigns for all their authors. Alas, not so. More than 1,500 business books are published each year. Only about ten percent of the authors behind these books receive much in the way of promotional support from their publishers. And very few of these had clauses in their contracts binding the publisher to provide it. In most cases, they got the support because the book got off to a quick start and the publisher wanted to maintain or build the sales momentum. I mention this here because many new authors believe that publicity plans constitute a negotiating point and should be in the contract.

An author needs tremendous leverage with a publisher to secure an upfront commitment to fund a book tour, a publicity campaign by a PR firm, or advertising of any kind. By all means request it, but it's naive to insist on it.

Do You Need a Lawyer?

New expert-authors from the business world often raise this question, even though they have seen attorneys kill their share of deals. It is reasonable, and arguably prudent, to have anything written by someone else's attorney reviewed by your attorney. Neither an editor nor your agent should object to that, and they should allow a reasonable period for the review.

Two caveats are in order, however: First, if an attorney lacks experience with book contracts, his review may be useless or worse. A publishing attorney is expensive, but in my opinion it makes more sense to have a specialist review the contract at his rate than it does to pay a "normal" rate for an inferior opinion. Second, attorneys have a simple way of keeping clients out of trouble on a contract. They tell you not to sign it. The more complex and expensive way is to negotiate better terms. This is where the billable hours can pile up.

Only you can decide whether to involve an attorney in your book deal. Whatever you decide, the key thing is to define clearly what is important to you and discuss it reasonably. If you like, you can sprinkle in a few phony demands to "give away" later, but my approach is to decide what I believe is fair, argue on the basis of fairness, and work toward those things.

The Authors Guild, one of the major associations for published writers, provides a free review by their legal department of any book contract extended to a member by a publisher. The service, which is first-rate, provides a written analysis that flags every provision that can work against the author. This doesn't mean you can get them all changed—after all, the Guild represents authors, not publishers—but you can better decide which provisions to negotiate. The service is for members only, but most regularly published authors and journalists are eligible for membership.

A Final Tip

This chapter strikes a balance between elementary and expert information, and outlines the tasks involved in getting an agent and a book contract. It also provides some "inside tips" to speed up the process. It cannot, however cover all aspects of finding an agent and landing a deal. For more information, consult relevant books among those listed in Appendix 2.

The fast track to a business book deal may seem slow at times. Finding an agent takes time. Writing a book proposal can take even longer. Yet an irresistible book proposal puts an author on the fastest possible track to publication. The next two chapters show how to write one.

4

Business Book Proposals that Sell the Sizzle

Convincing an Editor to Take the Plunge

I n its way, book publishing is an extremely democratic business. If you write a proposal that convinces an editor that your book has a) something to say, b) an audience that wants to hear it, and c) an author who can say it *and* sell it, you will get a book contract. You don't need to be a celebrity-CEO, a B-school professor, or a published author. Those things don't hurt, of course, but they're not necessary. You just need a compelling book proposal.

Many business people benefit from viewing the book proposal as the "business plan" or "product development plan" for the book. In presenting the content, target markets, competitive books, author's qualifications, and other material, the proposal provides information very similar to that in a business plan. The document also has the same goal—inspiring a group of people to back your idea and invest resources in bringing it to market with the hope of sharing in the profits. As an added benefit, the process of creating the table of contents and chapter summaries required for a book proposal provides you with a road map for the actual writing, after it has helped sell the book to a publisher.

As a sales tool, a book proposal is akin to other kinds of sales material. It describes the item being offered for sale, its features, benefits, competitive advantages, and other points of interest to potential buyers. It takes an enthusiastic tone and presents the product in the best light. As in most sales situations, the prospect is skeptical and needs reassurance. Therefore, the proposal must anticipate questions and objections, and address them. The best book proposals appeal to both the heart and the mind—the emotions and the intellect—to move the buyer toward the purchase decision.

The Buyer's Dilemma

Agents and editors ask the same question when evaluating a book proposal: Will this sell? The agent has to sell it to the editor. Then the editor has to sell it internally at the publishing house, which then has to sell it to the bookstores, which then sell it to the public.

Some publishers call their acquisitions editors "sponsoring editors." That's because an editor who likes a book proposal "sponsors" the project within the publishing house. Most editors cannot offer an advance and a contract without the approval of an editorial board composed of other editors and people from sales, marketing, publicity, and the business side of the house. The editor's role resembles that of a product champion in a company. The editor must get excited about your book, then get others committed to publishing it.

Therefore, a book proposal must answer the following questions:

- What's the main idea of the book? Is this a good idea? Is it original in concept or presentation, or both? Does it address a true need? Can this idea carry an entire book? Is the idea hot?

- What are the proposed contents? What is the content of each chapter?
- How is the material presented? Is it engaging and accessible, or serious and technical? Is this really a trade book, or is it a professional/technical book?
- What is the audience for this book? Does this audience buy books? How large is the potential audience? Can we reach the audience through our normal promotion and distribution channels?
- Where does this book fit in the marketplace? What books have been published on this subject? How is this one different? Does it fit our list and our current strategy?
- Does the author have the knowledge, expertise, and experience to come up with compelling material? Does she have credibility on this subject with the target audience?
- What can the author do to promote the book or boost its sales? Does she have a platform for promoting or selling this book? Is she media-savvy? Does she know people who will supply blurbs? Will she spend time and money promoting the book?
- Can the author write to professional standards and deliver the book she's promised? When will the manuscript be ready?

A proposal that follows the format described below will answer these questions for an editor and enable her to answer them for her colleagues. However, the proposal must also, like any sales document, sell the sizzle. While a simple Q&A approach to these questions could conceivably get you a contract, you'll fare better by drawing the editor into your world and demonstrating your ability to engage readers. That's part of selling the sizzle.

Editors are skeptics, but they are also romantics. (Yes, even business book editors.) Like writers, they have a streak of the gambler in them, and a gambler never abandons hope. So when an editor opens a proposal, he hopes to find the next *What Color Is Your Parachute?* or *In Search of Excellence*. He hopes to find a breakthrough book. He hopes to be knocked out by the author's originality, insight, flair for writing, and ability to inspire.

Let's do our best to fulfill the hopes of those business book editors wading through piles of unoriginal, uninsightful, ungrammatical, uninspired dreck. Let's get them excited. Let's make them pick up the phone and tell their editors-in-chief that they've just read a proposal that they *have to* make an offer on before someone else does.

The Parts of a Book Proposal

This chapter covers the front of the proposal. Chapter 5 covers the back of the proposal. The parts of the entire proposal are:

Front of the Proposal
- Executive Summary
- About the Book
- Target Audience and Competitive Books
- The Author
- The Writing Collaborator (if applicable)
- Author's Promotional Plan
- Specifications of the Book

Back of the Proposal
- Table of Contents of the Book
- Chapter Summaries
- Sample Chapter

The front sections of the proposal describe the book's concept, features, audience, competition, and authors. The back sections—table of contents, chapter summaries, and sample chapter—all present content proposed for the actual book.

The requirements for each section of the front of the proposal are as follows (the suggested page counts assume double-spaced text):

Executive Summary

Length: 1-2 pages

Like any executive summary, the one for a book proposal introduces the reader to the document by summing up its main points, in this case the concept, rationale, and target audience for the book, plus the author's background. But these summary pages must also get the editor excited. Moreover, they may be the only pages, aside from the book's table of contents, that people other than your editor actually read.

One useful approach to the executive summary follows these six steps:

1. Describe the situation that creates the need for the book
2. Present the book as the solution to this need
3. Summarize the concept of the book
4. Highlight things readers will learn or gain from the book
5. Note the target audience for the book
6. Mention the author and his qualifications

Try to follow this outline loosely. For instance, on the next page is a slightly shortened version of the executive summary from the proposal for *TechnoLeverage* by F. Michael Hruby.

We first try to startle the reader by asserting that most managers don't know how to exploit technology. Then we state that rich benefits accrue to managers who do know how to exploit it. In paragraph three, we introduce the book as the way to learn how to

Executive Summary

Technology drives business today. It creates business opportunities, transforms work, and boosts sales and profits. Yet most managers and professionals don't know how to exploit technology.

Most people approach technology as a tool, and that is fine as far as it goes. But rich possibilities open up to those who can *also* approach technology as a renewable source of business opportunities. Such a view is strategic rather than tactical, and dynamic rather than static. This view also never loses sight of financial realities.

We present this view in *TechnoLeverage: Using Technology-Based Strategy to Build Profit Machines*. This book fully integrates technology into an approach to the strategic issues that all managers face, including:

- What business are we in, and where are we going?
- What resources do we have, and how can we best use them?
- Who are our competitors, and what are they doing?
- How do we sustain growth and make more money?

TechnoLeverage is a call for *technology-based strategy*. For managers who apply this strategy, technology truly becomes the profit machine of the subtitle—because of the global scale, rapid growth, and huge margins inherent in well-managed technology.

We show readers how to develop and employ technology-based strategy. And that is just one of many insights that F. Michael Hruby, president of Technology Marketing Group, Inc., brings to readers in *TechnoLeverage*. In his twelve years at TMG, Mike Hruby has guided hundreds of companies to levels of performance they had not thought possible. With this book, he helps thousands more do the same.

do this. The bullets tie the book to common problems all managers face. Then, we herald the notion of technology-based strategy and finally, introduce the author.

It's easier to achieve conciseness in the executive summary if you've already developed a strong idea and positioning strategy. Although the idea and positioning will evolve as the proposal is written, the stronger they are at the outset, the easier the writing will flow.

Which raises an issue: Should you write the executive summary before or after you write the body of the proposal?

The answer is, write the proposal—and for that matter the book itself—in whatever order works best for you. Some authors like to have a draft of the executive summary as a kind of mission statement for the project, so they write one at the outset. Others prefer to have the proposal finished before knocking out the executive summary. It's a matter of personal style, although in collaborative situations having an executive summary as the mission statement makes sense. It's easier for a team to reach agreement on two pages than on fifty.

About the Book

Length: 3-6 pages

This section describes the concept of the book, its approach to the material, and the benefits it offers the reader. It answers the questions: Why this book? and Why now?

For a business how-to title, the best way to begin this section is to dramatize a problem, issue, or situation that the book helps readers address. For instance, in the proposal for *Business Is a Contact Sport*, About the Book began as shown in the example on the following page.

The section goes on to say that success still depends on managing those relationships skillfully and that this book shows readers how to do that.

For a book about a company, executive, or entrepreneur, open About the Book by portraying a scene from the story using action, dialogue, and description. Draw the reader into the narrative and then back off to describe the approach of the book. This creates more engagement than describing the approach and then portraying a scene.

Use the following phrases to help you develop topic sentences for paragraphs that will build a case for your book.

"Until now, executives and managers _____ _____." (Here you describe the sad state of affairs that executives and managers have been coping with until your book came along.)

"Several statistical facts highlight the seriousness of the situation our book addresses: _____.
(Here you insert numerical, or at least factual, evidence that the situation exists and is serious. For instance, for a book on leading change you could say, "According to _____ (name the source), two out of three organizational change initiatives fail."

With the principles and practices provided in _____ (title of your book) readers will be able to _____. (Here mention several improvements people will be able to make in their business lives after reading your book.)

"In _____ (title of your book) readers will learn: _____." (Here you provide three to five bullets on the best lessons in the book.)

The proposal in Appendix 1 presents a full About the Book section.

Strengthening the Case for Your Book

To make the rationale for publishing your book even more compelling:

- Quote statistics and cite sources, such as government studies, industry studies, the *New York Times*, the *Wall Street Journal*, major business magazines, and B-school reviews. Quoting a well-known authority can help the cause, as can other forms of name-dropping in a proposal.
- Find newspaper and magazine stories that show managers struggling to survive without the knowledge your book will provide. Use these as examples and cases and sources of quotes in the proposal.

- Note the wonderful things that have happened when companies (for example, your clients) have used the tools presented in your book. Cite market victories and performance records they have achieved.
- Position your book as riding a trend. This can be either a future trend for which there's credible evidence or a long-standing trend not covered by books, or at least not covered the way you cover it.

In a book proposal, you're selling an intangible, an idea. You must make the idea as real as possible for the reader. Otherwise, how can they justify committing real resources to publishing your book rather than another one?

Target Audience and Competitive Books

The target audience and competitive books, which are two subjects, could be covered in separate sections of the proposal rather than in subsections under one banner. However, the issues—Which readers does this book target? and Which books compete for those readers?—are closely linked. As you read the following material, refer occasionally to the market analysis in the sample proposal in Appendix 1 to see how the entire section works.

Target Audience
Length: 1-2 pages

Editors at most houses want trade books with potentially huge audiences. As we saw in Chapter 2, the size of the potential audience is strongly related to the nature and scope of the subject and to the idea and its positioning. That chapter explored ways of enriching ideas and positioning books for large audiences. In other words, targeting the audience began in developing the idea for the book.

Often a book will target several markets or distinct primary and secondary markets. Here are examples of multiple markets, quoted from business book proposals that sold:

- *Business Is a Contact Sport* targets a primary market of middle-to-senior level managers, entrepreneurs, and owners in companies of all sizes—and aspirants to these positions. Our secondary target market comprises human resources professionals, consultants, the nonprofit sector and business people in general, with this last group including employees at all levels and students and job seekers.

- *TechnoLeverage* targets managers, professionals, and entrepreneurs working in virtually any business that employs technology in any way. This includes makers and sellers of technology as well as purchasers and users of technology. This translates to a *potential* target market numbering well into hundreds of thousands of people.

- *Multipreneuring* aims for managerial and professional workers of all ages and in all stages of their careers. While we recognize that the baby-boom, pre-boom, and post-boom generations are in different stages of their lives and careers, we believe this book will appeal to all three cohorts. Why? Because the new working environment poses similar challenges regardless of one's age or career stage.

Do not forecast sales of the book based on capturing a certain percentage of the target market (or anything else). If possible, quote an impressive number that applies to your book's target market, for instance the number of home-based businesses in the United States or investors over sixty years of age. Government agencies and industry and professional associations are good sources of such statistics.

Fill out the picture of your target audience with 1) their motivation for buying your book, 2) information on their reading habits, or 3) the approach your book will take toward winning them. The following examples exemplify these three tactics.

Motivation of the Audience:

Business Is a Contact Sport: Our target readers are motivated by a desire to understand the "magic" by which some of us know "the right people" and develop rewarding relationships with them.

Reading Habits of the Audience:

TechnoLeverage: From a segmentation standpoint, our target audience includes readers of management books, strategy books, and technology books. Readers of books in any of these three categories represent a realistic, reachable audience for *TechnoLeverage* because the book blends management *and* strategy *and* technology.

Approach to the Audience:

Multipreneuring: Our book takes an inclusive approach toward all readers. Thus the examples and sources in the book include managers, employees, and professionals of all ages, both sexes, all colors, and from all organizational levels, as well as the self-employed, all of whom are also included in our target markets.

Anticipate barriers to reaching a wide audience. For instance, despite Title IX and the subsequent increase in women participating in sports in the past two decades, the authors believed *Business Is a Contact Sport* could be perceived as a book directed toward men. So the target market analysis included the following paragraph:

> Business Is a Contact Sport *is about managing business relationships. We therefore expect it to hold special appeal for*

women in that it focuses on the personal side of business and taps the concern that most women have with professional, as well as personal, relationships. We are fully aware that 60 to 70 percent of trade books are purchased by women.

Finally, mention any niche markets the book targets. Doing so may give the publicity people ideas for special promotions or book-club sales. It will also show that you are thinking hard about who your book can reach, which is what you should be thinking about as you write this section.

Competitive Books

Length: 3-5 pages

You can, if you like, avoid emphasizing the book's subgenre up to this point. This section, however, must define the category of book and its advantages vis-à-vis other books in that category. Editors think in terms of genres, subgenres, and their list needs. When there's confusion regarding the category of a proposed book, editors and salespeople ask questions such as: "What is this? A leadership book? A book for supervisors? Or a book about managing change?" Try to minimize such confusion.

The competitive analysis must:

- Show that you've researched the competition—other books on the subject—and that your book represents a contribution to the literature.
- Position your book attractively among other books on the subject, for the editor and for the sales, marketing, and publicity people.

How do you do this? By researching the books in your book's category. As you conduct this research, try to think about competitive books in the following two ways:

First, ask yourself: What's my book like? and How is it different? These are the very questions your editor will ask, consciously or subconsciously. Editors ask what it's like because they don't want to publish a book so radically new that it's unclassifiable. They ask how it's different because, while they want a recognizable book, they don't want one that's derivative. We'll look at ways of differentiating your book below, but first know where it stands in the scheme of things.

Second, kick off your shoes, put your feet up, and picture the titles that your target readers already have on their bookshelves. This directs you toward books in the right category while challenging you to imagine why they would buy yours too. Why would buyers of *Creativity in Business* also buy *Six Thinking Hats*? Why would someone read *The Entertainment Economy* and then *The Experience Economy*? *The Mind of the CEO* and then *Leadership IQ*? To answer these kinds of questions and understand the market, you must examine other books in your book's category.

Resources for Research

Several resources can help you identify books by category and learn enough about them to position your book in relation to them.

Amazon.com, bn.com, and other online bookstores are incredibly useful tools for book hunters. The ability to search a database of hundreds of thousands, even millions of books by title, words in the title, author, and key subject terms represents a quantum leap over hard-copy reference works. A search on key subject terms, that is, the topic of your book, will often deliver hundreds, even thousands, of titles. As of this writing, a search on "leadership" calls up 7,400 titles at Amazon.com and 8,800 at bn.com. The words "business leadership" yield 3,000 and 3,800, respectively. However, "executive coaching"—a fairly hot topic in business at the moment—accesses only four and thirty-one titles. The discrepancy between keyword searches on the two most widely used online bookstores can be significant. The keywords "business strategy" surface 233 titles at Amazon.com but more than eight times that number on bn.com.

When a search locates thousands of titles, narrow things down with a more finely tuned subject search or use key title-words instead. It's also useful to see which books people who bought books like yours also purchased—information that's provided automatically when you access a title at Amazon.com or bn.com.

Amazon's reviews, from the press and readers, also help. While some reader reviews are planted by friends of enterprising authors, you're not reading them for their opinions as much as for the book's content and approach. You'll quickly learn which books are too technical or too fluffy, too analytical or too anecdotal, or too impractical or too different to be truly competitive with your book.

Amazon's business best-seller list keeps you up on what's selling. It is skewed by bulk orders from companies, but you can correct for that to some extent by consulting Amazon's list of the best selling bulk-ordered books (most of which are business books). The online bookstore of Barnes and Nobel, bn.com, has its own set of features, which largely parallel Amazon.com's.

Finally, most business book publishers maintain their own sites, as indicated in Appendix 2. Publishers' online or hard-copy catalogs can be an excellent source of competitive titles and descriptive information. Most publishers will send their catalog on request or at least direct you to their Web site.

It's essential to augment visits to cyberspace with trips to brick-and-mortar bookstores. You will invariably find titles that you missed online, and get a sense of how books jockey for shelf space and for front-cover versus spine display.

Soundview Executive Book Summaries publishes what amount

to the CliffsNotes of the business book world. From over 1,200 submissions per year, the Soundview editors choose thirty titles for coverage in six-page summaries and scores of others for shorter reviews. The six-page summaries encapsulate the approach, structure, and major points of the book. Although Soundview covers a limited number of titles, they summarize or review a high percentage of the most popular ones. The company offers a subscription service, but you can also order stand-alone summaries for the two or three books that most directly compete with yours.

With a sheaf of research material, notes, and a few books in hand you are ready to begin your competitive comparison.

Compared with What?

The mix of books you compare yours with should include a few of the following:

- classics of the genre, preferably published within the past ten years
- recent best sellers in the genre
- original, respected books in the genre, even if they weren't best sellers.

You should also compare your book with some titles in separate but related categories to broaden the analysis and add interest, especially if your book straddles genres or occupies a small genre.

In a nice way, note the advantages of your book over the comparative titles. Success here depends on striking the right tone. Cite the strengths of other books, but also the gaps and limitations which your book addresses. For instance, a competitive analysis of a proposed book on marketing would probably unearth a competitive book that covers marketing products but not marketing services, or one that's strong on consumer marketing but weak on business-to-business marketing. Similarly, a competitive job hunting book may help readers analyze their strengths, weakness, and interests, but offer little on making contacts, handling interviews, and negotiating compensation. Or it may cover job search skills but omit some essential ones.

Identify knowledge gaps, instructional gaps, audiences not addressed. If a competing title focuses on one industry, your book may cut across industries. If another book focuses narrowly on its subject or audience, yours can broaden that coverage. If the competing title is broad in its coverage, yours can be more specific. Or your book may offer an updated perspective.

The following paragraphs draw useful comparisons between the proposed book and competitive titles:

- *Business Is a Contact Sport*: Improving customer relations has been the focus of many books. Among the more successful have been *The Loyalty Effect* by Frederick F. Reichheld, *Customer Loyalty: How to Earn It, How to Keep It* by Jill Griffin, and *Permission Marketing* by Seth Godin and Don Peppers. All of these books recommend the basic strategy of relationship marketing to win customers. In contrast, *Business Is a Contact Sport*, shows readers how to manage *all* business relationships, not just those with customers.

- *TechnoLeverage: TechnoLeverage* faces no true direct competition. But one recent book—*Inside the Tornado* by Geoffrey A. Moore—has staked out similar territory. *Tornado* resembles *TechnoLeverage* in that the author 1) realizes that technology presents special strategic issues and 2) gives readers a conceptual framework for addressing these issues. The similarities end there. First, *TechnoLeverage* covers all technology, not just computer technology. Second, we offer more solutions. Third, *Tornado* defines success as becoming the next Intel, Microsoft, or Motorola. But even companies with more modest ambitions need to know how to manage technology, and *TechnoLeverage* targets that broader market.

- *Multipreneuring:* The distinction between *Multipreneuring* and books on career change is worth exploring. Nena O'Neill's *Shifting Gears* is a good book on career change as are *Second Careers* by Caroline Bind and *In Transition* by Mary Lindley Burton and Richard A. Wedemeyer. Some 39,000,000 aging baby boomers have already reached, or soon will reach, the dark side of 40. Many of them will realize that they are not going to become CEO or division head, and for these people, career change makes sense. But without the skills of the multipreneur, they are going to encounter the same frustration, under-employment, and insecurity in their new careers that they faced in their old ones. *Multipreneuring* helps readers break that pattern.

Instead of touting your book as superior, try to show where it fits in the lineup. Your proposal may well be reviewed by editors of competing books, so there's no point in knocking them, particularly if they sold well. Just explain why a reader in your target audience would buy your book when all those other books on the subject have already been published.

This leads us to the heart of your positioning effort—your USP.

The Unique Selling Proposition

A business book proposal should present what marketers call the USP—the unique selling proposition. If you're not familiar with this advertising war horse, the USP is exactly what it sounds like: an exclusive feature or benefit that differentiates a product from others in its category *and* motivates people to buy it, rather than one of the others. Every book is unique in some way. That uniqueness must be pointed out to the editor.

Creating a USP

No two books on a subject have the same author, style, approach, and examples. The unique selling proposition therefore rests on one of these elements—or, more accurately, the unique combination of these elements.

In creating your selling proposition, be sure to consider the following attributes of your book:

- Benefits to your readers. Will they make money, accelerate their careers, grow their business faster, become more effective?
- Size and scope of the audience. For instance, a book may give general readers sophisticated coverage of a common subject, or tailor a "male" topic to the needs of business women.
- Sources of the material, such as original research, proprietary processes, or client case studies.
- Author's qualifications, including education, experience, affiliations, clients, accomplishments, and reputation.
- Author's platform and ability to reach a wide audience.

Here are sample statements of unique selling propositions, although they were not labeled as such in the proposals:

- *Business Is a Contact Sport:* Many current books present methods for maintaining a specific type of business relationship, most often with employees or customers. Other books cover relationships with suppliers, shareholders, boards of directors, the community, and the media. No other book we could find in (or out of) print presents a program for managing the full spectrum of business relationships.

- *TechnoLeverage:* Our book aims to shift people's thinking about management, strategy, and technology. We propose the first hard-hitting, engagingly written, commercially conceived business book that says: "Forget your markets and operations for a moment and focus on your technology, because that's the source of your competitiveness and growth. Learn how to use technology to make more money."

- *Multipreneuring:* Our book holds a unique advantage—our readers will learn how to develop the *total package* they need to succeed in the freelance economy. We cover the personal qualities, mind-set, skills, strategies, and tactics that everyone now needs in order to find work, develop opportunities, and execute projects.

Filling in the blanks that follow will help you write paragraphs to include in your competitive analysis:

> A number of books have taken _____ (the topic of your book) as their subject. Among the most recent notable titles are _____, _____ and _____ (titles of three books). Each of these, in its way, represents a real contribution. However, each of them also differs markedly from our book. (Then describe those differences.)
>
> Our survey of books in print revealed no directly competitive titles. There are however, several books that compete indirectly with _____ (title of your book). (Name those books and show why they are not directly competitive with yours.)

Here are two final hints for writing the Target Audience and Competitive Books section:

- While it's important to compare your book to at least one or two best sellers, avoid relying on "the usual suspects," such as the breakthrough books mentioned in Chapters 1 and 2. Some proposals mention best sellers totally unrelated to the proposed book's genre, which is useless, at best. Instead, find books in your category that have sold well.

- If you believe editors may misunderstand the type of book you're proposing, make the distinction two or three times. For instance, Mike Hruby felt that editors could mistake *TechnoLeverage* for a book on information technology when it's about how to use *any* technology to make money. The proposal clarified that point a few times.

Identifying the target audience and positioning the book among other titles are key tasks of the proposal. This section will not "write itself," so be prepared for some thorough research, clear thinking, and careful writing.

About the Author
Length: 1-2 pages

This section must answer the questions: Can the author write this book? and Once it's published, how can the author help us sell it?

To answer the first question, you must show that you have a) the knowledge and experience to generate great material and b) the ability to string together thousands of words in a way that people will want to read. The proposal itself, particularly the sample chapter, will do a lot to demonstrate that the material exists and that you (or your ghost) can write professionally.

To support the answer further, in About the Author include:

- current place of business and position
- former places of business and positions related to the book's topic
- accomplishments that have prepared you to write this book
- names, publishers, and dates of books you have written
- names of periodicals and newspapers that have published your work
- nature of any self-published material, such as newsletters, white papers, or executive briefings
- degrees earned
- client list, particularly well-known companies

To answer the second question—How can the author help us sell this book?—you must present yourself as someone with a "platform." If you are famous, or at least head a famous organization, or you are conducting seminars for 12,000 people a year, this section will be easy to write. If you lack such a platform, you must show that you have the ability, or at least the potential, to promote the book effectively.

Here are things to include:

- interviews you have given on radio and on broadcast and cable television
- publications in which you have been quoted
- speaking engagements and appearances (for instance, as a panelist) in front of business, professional, or civic groups
- workshops or seminars you have facilitated
- size and nature of your network of contacts, particularly media contacts
- if substantial, the size of the distribution list for your newsletter or other mailings
- activity on your Web site

The editor wants to know that you are "getting in front of people" or at least that you are willing and able to do so. If you have a good amount to say on this subject, say it in the Authors' Publicity Plan section (see below).

The Writing Collaborator

If a ghostwriter, co-author, or published author will be collaborating on the book, mention her separately, particularly if she has a business book track record. An alternative is to present the collaborator's background, stressing her writing credits, as the last part of the About the Authors section.

Author's Publicity Plan

Chapter 8 covers publicizing your book in depth, so we need not dwell on it here. The information in that chapter will help you write this section. If you fully intend to plan and fund a publicity and marketing campaign, outline the individual initiatives here in bullet points. If you have any way of moving books, such as seminars or speaking engagements, or will buy books at the author's discount and distribute them, mention that here as well. If on the other hand, you plan only to make yourself available for interviews with print and broadcast media and do some light promotion, mention that with as much positive spin as possible.

Authors' platforms and promotional skills now drive much of the business book trade. It is in your interest to think deeply about ways to generate interest in your book. Do research. Speak with book promoters. Consider your target readers and ways of reaching them. Include anything positive in the proposal that you reasonably can. Information on your promotion plans will help the editor sell the proposal to the publisher's sales, marketing, and publicity people.

Some new authors prefer to hold back in this area. If they are willing to spend their own time and money promoting the book, they reason, what incentive does the publisher have to do any promotion? Meanwhile, the publisher is thinking that if an author isn't willing to promote his own book, why should the publishing house promote it?

The answer to the second question is, of course, to sell more books. But publishers are famous for failing to promote their books. Again, Chapter 8 goes into promotion in detail. For now, two recommendations: First, understand that the sales of your book and its success as a marketing piece for your business depend on the effort you put into promoting it. Second, if you have an agent, discuss the whole issue of promoting the book with her early in the process.

Specifications of the Book

Length: 1 page

See the sample proposal in Appendix 2 for this page, which simply lists the book's format (hardcover, usually), length (60,000 to 65,000 words, usually), and manuscript delivery date.

The delivery date of the manuscript is the most important item here. Editors buy most business books about twelve to twenty-four months before the publication date. Again, allow nine months to a year to write the book if the introduction and sample chapter are complete and the book requires only light research. If the book is half-written, feel free to adjust the date accordingly. Remember, once the manuscript is completed, the publisher needs six to twelve months to produce and distribute the book.

Cover and Binding of the Proposal

Unlike manuscripts, proposals of the length suggested here are usually sent to publishers in bound form. Either GBC binding— the plastic "grabber" device named for the company that sells it— or the "coil" type will do. Avoid tape, perfect binding, report covers, and binders that come apart.

The cover of the proposal can be anything from a plain white sheet of paper listing the title and author's name to a full-color, professionally designed effort. Proposals with all types of covers sell, but a spiffy cover might grab the editor's attention and help her "see" the book more clearly. Follow your agent's guidance on proposal covers. And be sure to include the agent's name and contact information on the cover or the inside title page.

Final Tips

These general guidelines apply to the entire book proposal:

- Double space all text.

- Refer to your book in present tense. This creates the impression that the book exists. Although the editor knows it doesn't—the manuscript delivery date is well into the future—present tense makes it more real and lends immediacy to the writing.

- In the footer area, insert the page number and below that, in nine point type, the copyright line so it appears on every page: © copyright 2003 by Tom Gorman. (If you wish, use your own name instead of mine).

- Italicize the name of your book throughout the proposal. In the competitive books section, I underscore the comparative titles, even though italics would be more proper. I want my book to stand out.

- Certain companies have been used so often in proposals that their mere mention induces narcolepsy in editors. These include H-P, 3M, IBM, GE, Dell, Southwest Airlines, Nike,

Coca Cola, American Express, Microsoft, FedEx, Home Depot, Ben & Jerry's, and others famous for their leaders, cultures, business models, or track records. Mention them if you must, but approach them from a fresh angle. Better still, try to use other large but overlooked companies, foreign companies, or smaller, relatively unknown outfits.

- Understand that the public will not see your book proposal, so, if you must, you can use composite examples to support some points. Editors know this goes on and that authors simply want to avoid doing research on spec, although actual research would probably strengthen the proposal. In general, be as factual as possible because down the road it makes the writing easier and keeps fiction out of your non-fiction book.

This completes our tour of the front of the proposal. If you do your job well up to this point, the editor will know what kind of book you intend to write, who you expect to buy it, which books they tend to purchase, and what qualifies you to write and sell the book.

Chapter 5 shows how to develop and present a table of contents, chapter summaries, an introduction, and a sample chapter that will make an editor make an offer.

Sample Material Editors Can't Resist

Creating a Compelling Table of Contents and Chapter One

 aving read the front of the proposal, the editor is now excited about the prospect of publishing this book (or at least she hasn't stopped reading). The book has a solid premise and a great title. The target audience is large and will readily see the benefits of buying this book instead of, or in addition to, others on the subject. The author has credentials, credibility, and a platform.

Can this book be as great as it's cracked up to be?

The back of the proposal must answer that question "Yes!" Each remaining part of the proposal plays a vital role in providing that answer. These parts are:

- Table of Contents
- Chapter Summaries
- Sample Chapter

Even in these days of promotion-driven publishing, these sections are as important as the front of the proposal. Here's how to get them right.

Terrific Tables of Contents

The table of contents of the book is, along with the executive summary and About the Author, one of the sections editors read first. Like any table of contents, it conveys the book's structure and the author's approach to the material. It is the editor's first look at the actual book, and it's one of the first things that browsers see when they open the published volume.

Therefore, the table of contents must make a good impression. It has to intrigue the reader while being accessible, and promise a payoff while not asking him to work too hard. The reader—that is, the agent, editor, or consumer—must "get" the book quickly from the table of contents. Yet it can't be dull or dumbed down.

It's a lot to ask of one or two pages. Fortunately, we know it can be done because it has been done, often.

Let's Hit the Tables

One great table of contents—one that illustrates how seamlessly a book's title, structure, and contents can flow together—comes from *The Seven Habits of Highly Effective People*. The title couldn't be better. It promises, and it promises big: Develop these seven habits and you will become an effective person.

Perhaps you have already seen it, but even if you have, look again at the table of contents on the opposite page.

Stephen Covey packs a lot of information into this table of contents. However, he "chunks" the information into four parts and, of course, seven habits. The table promises payoffs—private victory, public victory, and renewal. It also indicates how these

The Seven Habits of Highly Effective People

Table of Contents

great things will happen, through principles such as personal vision, personal leadership, personal management, and so on.

Covey captures the reader's attention with intriguing concepts. For instance, "Inside-Out" at the beginning and "Inside-Out Again" at the end indicate that the reader will somehow learn how to work from the inside, out—a sensible and appealing idea. Also, that seventh habit, Sharpen the Saw, prompts a line of thought. A saw is a) a tool for b) serious work, which c) isn't sharpened often enough by most homeowners. The phrase Sharpen the Saw sums up the "principles of balanced self-renewal": To stay sharp, you occasionally must stop working. You must lead a balanced life.

Finally, the four-part structure—Paradigms and Principles, Private Victory, Public Victory, and Renewal—maps the author's approach to the material for the reader.

Combining chapter titles with brief explanations or expansions of each title is an excellent approach. Mike Hruby used this device in the table of contents in the proposal for *TechnoLeverage,* which I've reproduced here.

As both of these tables of contents show, creative writing adds value. Wording should be clever, but not so clever that you lose the reader. It's fine to use familiar phrases—Covey was not the first (or last) author to advise us to Think Win/Win, nor did Hruby coin the terms Future Perfect or The Winner's Circle—but such phrases must relate to the chapter contents, not just hang around trying to look good.

I've also included the table of contents from Emmett Murphy's *New York Times* Business Best Seller, *Leadership IQ.*

Murphy takes a different approach. By not explaining the chapter contents, he intrigues the reader with his leadership "types." He implicitly promises that a manager will, by reading this book, come to understand these types of leaders—and with the help of

TechnoLeverage

Table of Contents

Introduction

Leadership IQ

Table of Contents

Introduction

the self-assessment in the appendix, understand herself as a leader and improve her "Leadership IQ."

Developing the table of contents demands time and effort disproportionate to the real estate it occupies in the proposal or the book. It needs repeated tweaking and polishing. Although it may undergo further revision in the writing process, it's worth it to develop the best possible table of contents for the proposal. It will not only help land a contract, it will also generate a workable structure for the book, and structure stands among the tougher challenges in book development.

How It's Done

Developing the table of contents goes hand in hand with developing the idea of the book, so one or more of the following steps may already have been completed (or at least started) during the idea development phase:

1. Revisit the book idea and brainstorm around it
2. Evaluate and group the results of the brainstorm
3. Write provisional chapter titles
4. Find or choose a structure

These steps should be reiterated until you have provisional chapter titles and a workable structure. Switch the order of the steps if necessary. If you find a structure as you are doing Step 1, don't wait until Step 4 to write it down and start working with it.

Step 1. Revisit the Book Idea and Brainstorm Around It

A rich idea will throw off numerous related ideas. If you have not yet brainstormed around the central idea of your book to generate material, now's the time to get started.

What kind of material are you trying to generate? For a business how-to title, essential elements include principles, practices, procedures, programs, steps, cases, examples, quotations, old sayings, anecdotes, and images of people and situations related to the book's concept.

Pose questions to yourself. For instance, the question, "What would someone have to do to become a multipreneur?" eventually led to the following chapter titles for *Multipreneuring*:

- Add Value Constantly
- Act Like a Producer
- Manage Risk Aggressively
- Market Hard, Sell Soft
- Work Productively and Flexibly
- Exploit Technology
- Learn Continually
- Take Care of Business

These became the titles of Chapters 2 through 9 of the book.

Adding a first chapter, Adapting to the New Marketplace, and a tenth, Making the Transition, rounded out the table of contents.

Remember, as in any brainstorming exercise the goal here is quantity, not quality. Shoot for a high volume of material. Don't worry about whether it's any good. Don't ponder where it would go in the book. This step should produce raw material—a big pile of ideas. In fact, one of the best brainstorming methods is to write your ideas on index cards and make an actual pile of them.

Step 2. Evaluate and Group the Brainstormed Ideas

Having banished the internal critic that kills creativity, now you have to invite that critic back to the table. Take the brainstormed material and evaluate it for potential inclusion in the book. Keep anything that seems promising. This includes ideas that seem dull, as long as they might fit. A creative author can enliven dull ideas with novel nomenclature and vivid examples. Weed out any unrelated, impractical, nonsensical, or tasteless ideas. If there's no such material, then you probably weren't really brainstorming.

After evaluating them, group related ideas, principles, practices, procedures, sayings, and anecdotes in clusters. Some of these clusters, in some form, will become the chapters of the book. Work with the material in these groups. Refine and regroup as necessary. Move ideas around until you have between eight and fourteen piles of material.

Step 3. Write Provisional Chapter Titles

Once you have your groups, name them. Don't get hung up on finding the actual chapter titles too early in the process. If they pop up, great. If they don't, start with blandly descriptive titles. For example, for a book on selling, call the chapter on prospecting Prospecting. Later you can come up with something like Beating the Bushes and Banging the Drums, or whatever fits the book. For a book on leadership, call the chapter on developing a vision Developing a Vision. In a job hunting book, call the networking chapter Networking. Then you have something to wordsmith and polish.

If you want to be more creative in this step, go right ahead. But don't agonize over the final chapter titles until you have the chapter content defined. Keep in mind that it may take several iterations to generate and refine the material to bring it to that point.

Step 4. Find or Choose a Structure

For how-to business books, try to structure the material into about 250 published pages and eight to twelve chapters. That's just a guideline, of course. Business books of all lengths, word counts, and numbers of chapters have succeeded. In general, however, unless the material suggests an unconventional structure—say, 365 Ways to Have the Most Successful Year of Your Life—try a conventional one. Most editors want books with a straightforward format. They also want evidence that your idea can support a 250-page book. Aside from occasional novelty books like *The One Minute Manager* and *Who Moved My Cheese?*, most business books fit that profile.

In a 60,000-word, twelve-chapter book, the chapters will average 5,000 words each. The word count in the chapters will drop a bit if the book has an introduction and a preface or foreword, which we'll discuss later in this chapter. As a practical matter, all of these (and the appendix, if you include one) are calculated in the book's word count.

In most business books, Chapter 1 lays out the author's world view. It might portray the inefficiencies in some area of business or dramatize the plight of those who lack the skills presented in the book. It then proceeds to introduce the author's solution, program, or skill set. This chapter must engage the reader while presenting the author's program and "selling" it.

The final chapter often delivers a "call to arms" or similar inspiration to the reader. Or it may look into the future. Often it examines another application of the author's wisdom—at the global level or in personal life, for instance.

Here's another way of looking at it: In business how-to/self-help books, Chapter 1 could almost always be called Getting Started. The final chapter could usually be called Putting It All Together. These are not recommended titles because they've become clichés. But, regarding the actual chapter content, the point stands.

If the first and final chapters are bookends (sorry), what goes between them? The author's core material. This might consist of mindsets and skills, tools and techniques, principles and practices, or a process expressed in steps, stages, or phases. It might be some combination of these. Whatever the core content, it must be presented in a logical sequence. The sequence may lead the reader through higher levels of, for example, leadership proficiency. It may take the reader through increasingly difficult or complex steps—say, in developing a new company culture or closing sales that require multiple approvals.

The chapters may also be organized into parts, if it helps the reader. For instance, the chapters of *Multipreneuring* were organized into four parts as shown here.

To get an idea of the incredible range of structural options at your disposal, visit a few bookstores and check out tables of contents in their business book sections. What looks inviting on paper? Which books use parts to chunk the chapters? When they do, does it add clarity? Which devices capture your attention and help you see what the book is about? Which ones cause confusion or put you off? What works?

Take note of approaches that might suit your book. Don't be afraid to look beyond the genre of the book you are writing. Some devices work well across categories. And while you're at it, visit

Multipreneuring

Table of Contents

Introduction

Part One
The Multipreneurial Response to Change

1. Adapting to the New Marketplace

Part Two
The Principles of Multipreneuring

2. Add Value Constantly
3. Manage Risk Aggressively
4. Work Productively and Flexibly
5. Learn Continually

Part Three
The Practices of Multipreneuring

6. Act Like a Producer
7. Market Hard, Sell Soft
8. Exploit Technology
9. Take Care of Business

Part Four
The Transition to Multipreneuring

10. Making the Transition

online bookstores. Many of their books offer access to the table of contents.

If this all sounds formulaic, please know that readers rarely notice the structure of a book. Did you consciously think about the structure of this book? Most readers don't give it a thought—unless it's not working. They want information, and as long as it's clearly presented, they don't care about the structure of a book or where it came from. Nor should they.

Remember too that almost all literary forms, by definition, have structural conventions. The three-act play, the sonnet, the haiku, the thriller, the romance—all follow formulas. Upon examination, so do business how-to books.

Beyond How-To

Structural considerations also arise in planning business books outside the how-to genre. Company stories require a dramatic arc, one that extends from the opening chapter—an introduction to the company and its key players—to the closing chapter—the denouement.

The intervening chapters must portray, through a series of stake-raising events, the company's rise, or rise and fall, or rise and fall and rise. These events will likely include new hires, expansion efforts, product launches, sales campaigns, acquisitions, competitive threats, and setbacks and failures. Celebrity-CEO books use a similar structure but are more anecdotal in approach and more personal in tone.

Study the tables of contents of books in the relevant genre. Try a few different approaches and ask people you know for feedback. When you hit a wall, put the material aside for a few days and let your subconscious work it out. The pieces may well come together when you return to the task. Keep at it. If the book idea is strong and the material plentiful, diligent effort will eventually produce the perfect table of contents for your book.

Chapter Summaries that Sing

Having seen the table of contents, the editor now wants to see the content of those wonderfully named chapters. This is where chapter summaries come in.

Each chapter requires a summary. For almost all business books, these should be no more than one page each. Some very effective book proposals use one-paragraph chapter summaries. However, if a proposal provides scant information on the actual contents of the chapters, editors may say, "We can't really see the book," or "Why are these two chapters in here?"

The template on the following page heads off such comments. It gives each chapter one page, and guides an author to write chapter summaries that:

- explain why each chapter is in the book
- convey the content of each chapter
- underscore each chapter's take-away value

Summaries developed with this template deliver maximum impact to readers who skim. They can choose to read the box at the top of the page, the bullets at the bottom, a paragraph or two, or the whole page.

The sample book proposal in Appendix 1, contains actual summaries from a proposal that sold. Referring to several of these summaries—particularly those for Chapters 2, 3, 6, 8, 9 and 12—will show how this template works in practice. The other chapter summaries show how the material in the paragraphs can vary in content and presentation. This sample proposal is not presented as an industry standard in terms of approach or format. It is simply an approach and format that has worked for me and my clients.

The most common mistake new authors make in chapter summaries is failing to dramatize the material. Showing a specific instance of poor communication or new product failure in

Chapter Summary Template

Chapter Number
Chapter Title
Chapter Subtitle, If Any

> *In this box, single-spaced and in italics, write a "teaser" summary of the chapter. This should be one to three breezy sentences on why this chapter is included or why readers will find it interesting.*

The first paragraph *shows* the editor the need for this chapter. It dramatizes a situation where the chapter's material applies. *For instance*, if the chapter showed managers how to improve their communication skills, the author could portray a manager having to communicate a difficult message to an employee, supplier, or group or show a manager communicating poorly and drawing forth the logical response ("Gee, Diane really got angry").

The second paragraph *tells* the editor about the chapter's benefits. This paragraph should follow the preceding one in a there's-the-problem, here's-the-solution fashion. *For example*, for communication skills, this paragraph could say: "Few managers consistently plan before they communicate, but good communication requires planning. In planning, a manager considers the message he wants to deliver, the people he wants to deliver it to, ways of delivering it, and potential responses. When managers plan even routine communications, they strengthen relationships with their people and get better results."

Then three bullets describe the chapter's lessons or high points. *For example*:

Here readers learn how to:
- Assess their communication skills
- Match their message and medium to their audience
- Acknowledge unpleasant realities, while emphasizing the positives.

that first paragraph will engage the reader. Bland assertions about the damage caused by poor communication or slipshod product rollouts won't. That first paragraph must show, not tell. Show people grumbling about a manager who communicates badly. Show the blood on the floor of the marketing department after a failed product launch. Bring the material to life and pull the reader into it.

Journalists use a dramatic "lead"—a specific incident—to pull readers into a newspaper or magazine article. For instance, a piece on poor communication might begin with a tyrannical boss publicly berating an underling. An article on new product failure might start by describing a botched roll-out for a new snack food. Specific details create mental images of people doing things. They generate more emotional involvement than a bunch of facts ever could.

As noted in Chapter 4, you can use real-life situations or create composite examples and cases. The more factual examples you use, the better. Cases from real life often have a you-can't-make-this-stuff-up quality. Use the chapter summaries to give the editor a taste of your experience, war stories, and case histories and to show that you can put them to good use.

Writing the chapter summaries can lead to some fine- (or not-so-fine) tuning of your book's structure. You may not have as much material for a certain chapter as you thought you did. Or perhaps you have enough content on a topic to fill two chapters. Material that looked good in the brainstorming phase may prove unusable. This is a normal part of book development.

One word of caution: If you find that you're not going to have enough material for a chapter and you don't see a way to develop that material, delete the chapter. Delete it even if it sounds cool and you love it. Why? Because that chapter may just turn out to be the one the editor flips for and definitely wants in the book. If that happens, you may find yourself trying to write out of thin air in a nonfiction book—a practice technically known as "slinging it." This practice is always frustrating, usually futile, and often dangerous to one's project (or, worse, integrity). Avoid trouble. If there won't be enough material to support a chapter, let it go.

Beyond How-To, Again

So far our discussion has been geared mainly to business how-to books. What if you're writing in a different genre? With minor adjustments, the same chapter summary template can still serve you well. Here's how you might do a chapter summary for a book on a company or an executive, for example:

- In the italicized box, show how this chapter moves the story forward. Write two or three lines that maintain the narrative momentum by taking the reader to the peak or valley covered in that chapter.
- The first paragraph can compress a key scene from the chapter, and the second could place that scene in context. For instance, first show the CEO arguing with his investment bankers over the cost of an acquisition. Then the second paragraph could say, "Cash-strapped Acme Corp. needed this acquisition in order to survive. The question was, Where would the money for the acquisition come from?" and briefly elaborate that theme.
- The three bullets could describe three key developments in the chapter. Or they could outline the chapter's narrative structure, cite the three major scenes, or explain the impact of the chapter on the reader. Or you could eliminate the bullets. That's allowed too.

As with all of the guidelines in this book, adapt the template to your needs. Twist it to fit the material and to keep editors reading.

A template should not draw attention to itself, although readers will quickly realize that the box at the top introduces the chapter and the bullets at the bottom outline its benefits. Vary your language in those sections to avoid sounding cardboard-cutout. For instance, the summaries in Appendix 1 employ various phrases to introduce the bullets at the bottom of the page:

- In this chapter, we show readers...
- Here we examine...
- This chapter demonstrates...
- Here readers will learn...
- In this chapter, we...

Variety keeps boredom at bay.

Taken together, the chapter summaries convey the shape and scope of the book. They help the editor envision the book. Ultimately, the author and editor build a common vision of the book. Although in some cases the editor buys the author's vision wholesale, a shared vision usually develops through an exchange of ideas aimed at sharpening the book's focus. Developing and refining your chapter summaries at the beginning strengthens your vision of the book. The stronger your vision, the better you will be able to convey it, defend it, and, when necessary, alter it without undermining it.

A Sample Chapter that Closes the Deal

The sex-and-glitz novelist Harold Robbins famously landed a $1 million advance just for submitting the title of *The Adventurers* to his publisher. When dealing with less exalted literary figures, editors want to see what they are buying. They want an indication that the proposal represents more than wild-eyed promises from an author who's written too much marketing copy.

The sample chapter shifts the editor's focus from the pitch to the product. Up to this point, although it's written in present tense, the proposal explains what the author will do and how great the book will be. Even the chapter summaries provide mere glimpses of wonderful things to come. The sample chapter is a slice of the actual book. As such, it must close the deal.

Closing the deal means sustaining the level of quality established so far in the proposal. Editors quickly notice disparities between the promise and the payoff. So, in the front of the proposal, avoid discussing anything that you can't deliver. Be enthusiastic, but don't overpromise. Then, in the sample chapter (which should be Chapter 1) smoothly shift from describing the material to delivering it.

Benefits of the Sample Chapter

In addition to clinching the deal, the sample chapter holds several benefits for the author.

First, it gives the author's agent more leverage with the publisher. Some authors who could get a deal without a sample chapter write one anyway. Why? Because then the publisher cannot use the lack of a well-written sample chapter to justify a low advance. Without a sample chapter, an editor can say, "Well, there's not much here. But we like the idea, so we're willing to risk a few bucks on it." A solid sample chapter supports the agent's efforts and helps the editor sell the project to her colleagues.

Second, writing the sample chapter helps the author gauge the time and effort needed to write the manuscript. No matter how things have gone up to this point, the book calls for a different type and amount of writing than the proposal. Issues such as structuring the chapter, allocating material, and finding a tone for the book all arise. The sample chapter forces the author to start grappling with these issues.

Third, the sample chapter exposes authors and collaborators more deeply to one another's working methods. If writing partners are incompatible, it's best that they figure that out before they sign a book contract. If they are compatible, they will start to develop efficient ways of working on the manuscript.

Finally, if the author cannot write the sample chapter, the project's prospects are dim. Some ideas pitch beautifully but don't pan out. Material or motivation may be lacking, or the book's time may have passed. That said, seasoned authors know that some resistance to beginning a book is natural, and not necessarily a cause for panic. The "shakedown cruise" of the sample chapter enables them to come to grips with any doubts, and either overcome them or abandon the project.

If the book does turn out to be unwritable as things stand, consider the alternatives. The project may be salvageable. A lack of material may simply indicate a need for more research. A lack of motivation or belief in the project might evaporate with a reassessment of the shape, scope, or content of the book. Alternatively, such a reassessment may point toward a better way of presenting the subject to readers. A topic that can't support a book might work nicely in a newsletter, executive briefing, magazine article, or series of articles.

Thus, even authors who can get a book contract without a sample chapter might wind up with better deals, easier starts, and fewer fruitless projects if they included one.

Getting Chapter One Done

Reading a pop business book should not be a chore or a bore. This doesn't mean you should pepper the text with sex scenes or slapstick comedy. It means that the writing should be smooth and engaging. Many of the guidelines regarding the chapter summaries—dramatize, be specific, use examples—apply to the sample chapter. (So do the more detailed guidelines in the next chapter, which covers writing the manuscript.)

Chapter 1 is usually one of the most enjoyable and easily written chapters in the book because of the "overview" nature of the material. In a business how-to or trend book, it presents the author's worldview. The author demonstrates that companies and people would be far better off if they possessed the knowledge and skills contained in the chapters to follow. Or he shows that the trend is transforming the way the world does business, and explains why this is so and what to do about it.

Aside from "hooking" the reader and explaining your worldview and program, Chapter 1 can accomplish several things:

- If you have a contrarian viewpoint, you can cite evidence and sources that support that viewpoint. Otherwise, beware: A pontificating or bitter tone may mar the writing.

- Similarly, if your book marks a departure from accepted practice charted in another author's book, you can deal with that in Chapter 1. In his superb *Getting Things Done*, David Allen uses Chapter 1 to set the stage by reminding us how busy we all are. He also notes that the old method of time management—A, B, and C priorities and to-do lists—is passé. (That method was popularized by the above-mentioned best seller, *How to Get Control of Your Time and Life*.)

- If you have written a previous book on a similar subject, use Chapter 1 to place the two books in context. If your current book builds on the previous one, you can summarize the earlier material here. In *Journey to the Emerald City*, Roger Connors and Tom Smith reprised key features of their first book, *The Oz Principle*, in Chapter 1. Taking a different tack, Geoffrey Moore used Chapter 1 of *Inside the Tornado* as an introduction to his new ideas, then used Chapter 2 to summarize his previous book, *Crossing the Chasm*.

- Any intricate disclaimers or explanations should go into Chapter 1, unless they've been covered in the introduction. The excellent *The Innovator's Dilemma* by Clayton Christensen shows how to manage in an era of disruptive technologies. However, the book rests on research done in one industry—hard disk drives. The first chapter presents "insights from the hard disk drive industry" and explains that "Few industries offer researchers the same opportunities…" In this way, a potential liability—research into a single industry—was turned into an asset.

Too often Chapter 1 belabors the need for the book or dwells too long on the situation that prompted the author to write it. One sign of this error is taking two chapters to "set the stage" instead of one. New business book authors often feel they need to paint a gruesome picture of how bad things are in the first chapter, and then present the solution in the second chapter. Avoid this mistake by presenting the need for the program *and* the program in the first chapter.

Similarly some narrative nonfiction books on companies or personalities spend the first chapter on deep background—for instance, the history of the industry—instead of plunging the reader into the action.

Business book readers "get it" very quickly and want things to move along. Many business people read for practical ends rather than for pleasure. We read biography, but often for lessons in leadership or deal-making. Literary fiction and poetry tops the reading list of few business people. So set things up quickly, use real-life examples liberally, and tell the reader *what* he should do and *how* he should do it. Be sparing with *why* he should do it.

Appendix 2 contains a full proposal except for the sample chapter because there's no real "formula" for writing a chapter of a book. Read a few first chapters from books that worked and you will see that each one, in its own way, engages the reader, explains the author's point of view, and sets up the rest of the book. Do that in your sample chapter (with help from Chapter 6) and your book proposal will be complete.

To Research or Not Research

In most cases, there's no way of being certain that a book proposal will sell. That being the case, should you invest time, money, and effort beyond the thinking and writing needed to create a solid sales document? Should you commission research? Should you conduct interviews? Should you do everything for the sample chapter that you would do for the actual chapter?

In general, the answer to these questions is "No"—or "No, but..." Editors understand that a sample chapter is just that, a sample. As long as the piece demonstrates command of the material and an ability to write well, it will probably do the job. But in most cases, a *bit* of research (beyond that on competitive books) markedly improves the sample chapter. Professional authors and ghosts typically research several newspapers, magazines, and Web sites for their proposals. This boosts their knowledge and unearths examples that support their points. Light research usually adds significant value to the proposal at a reasonable cost in time and effort.

Have We Been Introduced?

A book proposal with a sample chapter will work without including an introduction to the book. However, many proposals include one anyway. An introduction before the sample chapter allows for a little extra positioning and selling in the proposal because it can be looser and more personal in tone than the sample chapter. It serves a similar purpose in the book itself.

An introduction enables you to:

- Answer the question, "Who should read this book?"
- Explain the need for another book on the subject.
- Mention your background and your reasons for writing the book.
- Clarify anything new or potentially confusing. For example, if you have a "mystery title" that prompts browsers to open the book, the introduction can explain its meaning.
- Orient the reader to the book's approach and structure, instead of doing so in the first chapter. For instance, if you want to have a ten-chapter book that shows the reader how to acquire ten skills, you can explain your approach and the book's structure in the introduction and then devote all of Chapter 1 to the first skill.

Moreover, someone browsing in a bookstore often turns to the introduction first. If you can hook that reader with a powerful rationale or the promise of transformation, why not?

The introduction should be about 800 to 1,600 words. As for what those words should be, again, we'll examine business book writing from the "writing" standpoint in the next chapter.

What About a Preface or Foreword?

The preface and foreword are short pieces—usually less than a thousand words—that precede the introduction, and it's rare to find them both in one book. What's the difference between them? In general, the author writes the preface; someone else writes a foreword.

An author can use the preface to cite his reasons for writing the book, his sources or research methodology, or his earlier work that led up to the book. If the book won't feature an acknowledgments page, the acknowledgments can go into the preface. A preface works particularly well for subsequent editions of a book, enabling the author to mention the reasons for the new edition and the major changes from the preceding one. The author's name usually goes after the preface.

A foreword bears the name of the person who wrote it and points out why the book is valuable and important. To encourage potential readers to buy the book, the writer of the foreword often emphasizes the author's accomplishments, qualifications, and expertise.

A commitment from a famous individual to write a foreword can help you get a deal or at least impress an editor. Editors often suggest that unknown authors secure such a commitment, but most find the task difficult to impossible. You have to know someone famous and the person usually wants to see the manuscript or a partial manuscript before agreeing to write anything. Although the proposal doesn't require a preface or foreword, if you have a commitment from someone to write a foreword, do point that out.

On to the Writing

Completing a book proposal represents a major accomplishment. If done well and represented by a good agent, it should result in a book contract. If it does get you a contract, however, you must then write the book. On good days writing a book is fun, but not every day is a good day. Fortunately, as the next chapter demonstrates, every day of writing can at least be productive.

Sixty Thousand Sparkling Words

Getting it Down, and Getting it Right

 ou've targeted your audience, refined your message, marshaled your material, developed a structure, drafted a chapter, and found a publisher. You are now positioned to write the book. In other words, a large project lies ahead.

This chapter provides guidance for people facing that project. It does not explain how to write clear prose or how to correct grammar errors. Other books do that, and Appendix 2 lists several excellent ones. This chapter focuses on writing the business book, on approaches and devices that authors use to effectively present this type of material to readers. Although some of the guidance I will be offering applies to other types of books as well, it is geared to the needs of the business book author. It assumes an understanding of English grammar and composition, and the ability to write clearly.

Planning the Project

With luck, the manuscript delivery date in the book proposal has not been pushed up too far. As noted, an editor occasionally wants a book before the proposed date. If you're on an unreasonably short deadline, that's a problem. We'll address that and other problems in Chapter 7.

Regardless of the deadline, start developing a detailed plan for researching and writing the book, if you haven't already done so, *as soon as you accept the publisher's offer*. When you've completed the plan, start the actual research and writing immediately. If you wait for the contract to get out of the publisher's legal department, which could take one to six months, you will wind up hopelessly behind schedule.

The project plan for the book depends on the scope and type of research required, the skills and schedules of your collaborators, and competing claims on your time. The absence of research, collaborators, or competing claims simplifies planning.

Research may be primary (mail or telephone surveys or interviews conducted by you, your firm, or a vendor) or secondary (information garnered from newspapers, periodicals, books, or Web sites). Many new writers wonder whether it's best to complete all research before they begin writing or to research chapter by chapter as they write the book. While the best method depends on the author and the project, it's generally better to do most of the research before you begin writing. That way, you have all your material at hand. You'll be able to see the full scope of the book, making it less likely that you'll discover, well into the project, overlooked topics that should have been covered in the early chapters. However, if each chapter has its own very distinct research requirements, it's fine to research them one by one as you write the book. In practice, combining the two approaches often works best. Research before writing helps refine your vision of the book.

Research as you write lets you fill in holes and provides a break from writing.

Schedule research realistically and with long lead times. Interview subjects can be tough to contact, so don't wait: Call them soon after you have a deal. Some who initially refuse to take part in the project may yield to persistent but polite entreaties to do so, but you have to have enough time to exercise persistence.

Collaborators both help and hinder the writing process. They help to the extent that they provide skills that you lack and free you for other tasks. They hinder to the extent that they need to be taught about your business and book, and to the extent that they require supervision and review of their work. On balance though, a partner who understands his role and performs it well makes the process easier. Writing a book can be lonely work for those not accustomed to solitary pursuits. A collaborator reduces that loneliness as well as the workload. The key task is getting your partner's input and buy-in on the project plan.

Competing claims on your time are the thorniest aspect of planning. In practice, people who have full-time jobs and commit to writing a book sacrifice social, personal, and family time. (That's why authors acknowledge the "support and understanding" of their spouses, children, and friends in their books.)

Resist the temptation to overschedule in the belief that somehow you'll find a way to write the book quickly without undermining your other business activities, relationships, or health. Also, schedule time between writing and revising in order to get the distance you need to approach the draft with fresh eyes. During that time, research or write the next chapter. Working at a reasonable pace improves the quality of the book as well as the quality of your life.

For an organized, motivated author, six person-months represents a reasonable minimum time commitment for writing the book. This represents total person-hours, not elapsed time, and breaks down to a thousand hours, or twenty-five forty-hour weeks. It also breaks down to four hours of research, outlining, writing, rewriting, and editing time per published page of a 250-page book. For planning and control purposes, allocate twenty-five percent of this time to research and preparation, twenty-five percent to writing the draft, and fifty percent to rewriting, revising and editing. This allocation will vary by author and project, but a quarter, a quarter, and a half—or a third, a third, and a third—is a good rule of thumb.

Book editors, bless 'em, leave authors to their own devices. They want to see a chapter or two to ensure that things are off to a good start. After that, most will wait patiently for delivery of the first third or half of the manuscript, as agreed. If you don't hear from your editor, it's not for lack of interest. She is off doing her job and letting you do yours.

Ready, Set, Write

A pure information product, such as a market survey or an industry study, delivers facts. The reader buys these facts, at a multiple of the price of a trade book, to support a specific business decision. Most trade books don't deliver this type of decision-specific information. A book's content may be equally or more important, but it is not decision-specific in the same sense. Thus, the reader may not be as motivated to read it. With lower motivation, the reader will be less tolerant of unclear prose or boring content. If he encounters them, he'll put the book down and pick up a magazine, turn on the television, or surf the Web.

Books must entertain readers as they inform them. That's where you, the author, come in. You must engage the reader, or at least keep her interested, in order to deliver full value and customer satisfaction (and generate the word-of-mouth so essential to a book's success). Chapter 5 mentioned ways of engaging the reader. This chapter examines these and other "tools of engagement" more closely. They include:

- style
- tone
- examples and cases
- similes, analogies, and metaphors
- narrative devices
- facts and figures
- diagrams, charts, and illustrations
- humor
- format

Let's focus individually on each of these writerly tools.

Say It with Style

Business books require a clear, readable, smooth style of writing. One reader likened the writing in a business book he enjoyed as being akin to "hearing someone at my shoulder, talking in my ear." It's an interesting comparison because writing does register on the reader's internal ear. Choppy writing grates on the ear. Stuffy writing induces snoozing.

Read aloud to yourself from several business books. Listen for the writer's voice, his style of writing. Does it drone? Or does it seem as if he's talking to you in a lively manner?

Also, notice the length of the words and sentences in the book. Believe it or not, most mass-market material is written at high school grade levels—or lower. According to Deborah Dumaine's excellent guide to business writing, *Write to the Top*, the *New York Times* is written at a tenth-grade level, the *Wall Street Journal* at an eleventh-grade level, *Time* and *Business Week* at a tenth-grade level, *USA Today* at a seventh-grade level, and *People* at a sixth-grade level. Applying Fry's Readability Index, the tool Dumaine uses, to several popular business books yields the following grade levels:

The Seven Habits of Highly Effective People 10
The Millionaire Next Door 9
Write to the Top 9
The Complete Idiot's Guide to MBA Basics 8
Jack: Straight from the Gut 7

Is this to imply that Jack Welch is writing down to his audience? No, only that he wants to reach as many readers as *People* and *USA Today*. His (and his collaborator's) writing has a down-to-earth style that is clearly intentional and in keeping with the title of the book. By the way, the book you are reading at the moment is written at a tenth-grade level.

Fry's Readability Index, like most such indexes, is based on the average number of words per sentence and the average number of syllables per word in the text. The higher those averages, the higher the grade level and the tougher the read. The lower those averages, the easier the read. I've found Fry's Graph for Estimating Readability, developed by Dr. Edward Fry, formerly of Rutgers University, so useful that I've included it here. If you use it, apply it to three different samples of the text for best results. The readability indexes and grade levels included in word processing software are also useful. However, the hands-on experience of using this chart generates greater awareness of what makes writing "sound" the way it does. (Most writers find the grammar checkers in word processors less useful, but they do flag long sentences.).

How does this relate to style? Word length and sentence length largely determine style. Polysyllabic words and circumlocutory sentences are the mark of an academic writing style. This may

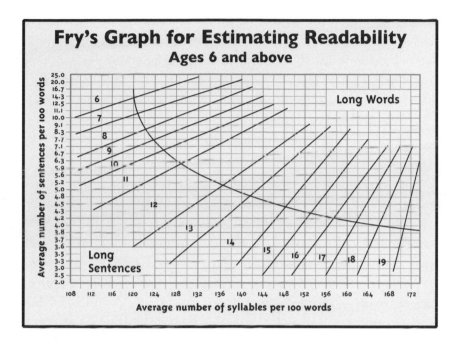

Fry's Graph for Estimating Readability
Ages 6 and above

Average number of sentences per 100 words

25.0
20.0
16.7
14.3
12.5
11.1
10.0
9.1
8.3
7.7
7.1
6.7
6.3
5.9
5.6
5.2
5.0
4.8
4.5
4.3
4.2
4.0
3.8
3.7
3.6
3.5
3.3
3.0
2.5
2.0

6
7
8
9
10
11
12
13
14
15
16
17
18
19

Long Words

Long Sentences

108 112 116 120 124 128 132 136 140 144 148 152 156 160 164 168 172

Average number of syllables per 100 words

have created the idea that big words and long sentences "sound smart." However, an academic style has no place in business books, as the reading levels just noted indicate. Again, I'm not talking about "writing down" to your audience. That's more an issue of tone than style. Rather it means writing in plain English using active voice and sentences of reasonable length. Sentence length should vary, but rarely extend beyond thirty words. An *average* sentence length of about fifteen mostly short words translates to the ninth grade level, which is *Write to the Top*'s recommendation for business letters and memos.

Use a straightforward, conversational style. Say it on paper the way you would to a friend sitting across from you. If this proves difficult, just write the way you normally would even if it seems too formal or dry or disjointed. Don't agonize over it. You can fix it later. Get it down, then get it right. The true style of a book doesn't emerge until the editing phase anyway. That's when, after you've written a draft, you go back and delete and rewrite words and sentences until they sound just right. The key point is that you don't want readers tripping over words or reading passages twice. You don't even want them thinking about your writing style. You want them thinking about your message.

Strike the Right Tone

Tone is a bit like style, but it emerges from the author's intellectual and emotional approach to the material and the reader. Some writers employ a judgmental or condescending tone without even knowing it. One author I worked with habitually used phrases such as, "Intelligent managers realize..." and "Laziness or stupidity lead many companies to..." The first phrase may place the reader in the unintelligent group, where he no doubt would rather not be. The second phrase sounds harsh. It's best to attribute shortcomings to inexperience.

A pontificating or lecturing tone can be harder to avoid, particularly in a business how-to book. How does an expert dispensing advice avoid a superior tone? By using the friendly, positive, informal tone that most of us use in face-to-face conversation. Such communication characterizes American business people, who are known for it internationally. Some European, Asian, and South American business people find it strange or annoying at first, but most soon realize that an American's informal, straight-talking attitude implies no disrespect and quickly fosters camaraderie and teamwork. Try for that approach on paper.

Study the tone of successful business books. Then go and do likewise. Avoid words and phrases such as "obviously," "stupid," "as anyone could see," and "as they should have known." Consider the reader (and everyone mentioned in your book) to be as savvy as yourself, and you'll strike the right tone.

Use Examples and Cases

Nothing enlivens a business book more than real-life examples and cases. Nothing deadens one more than their absence. Examples and cases put flesh and blood on the concepts, principles, and practices you're presenting to the reader. In a business how-to book, they show the ideas in action and enhance your credibility. A business narrative about a company or person is virtually one long string of "examples" and "cases."

Examples and cases come from:

- your own experience
- primary research
- secondary research
- composites you create

Cases from your own experience are generally the most powerful. They are uniquely yours and therefore new to the reader. You can discuss them intimately and in great detail because you were there. To get the most from your experiences, you must plan ahead and know how to present and apply them in a book.

Planning ahead ideally means gathering material long before you start writing the book. This may entail developing client case-studies, keeping a journal, or recording an oral history as you build a business or progress in a career. It means securing permission from customers to use their names, although this isn't always possible. Few clients want to admit that they were floundering until you came along with your product or paradigm. Yet many will cooperate if they know they'll be portrayed in a positive light.

Here are guidelines for presenting examples and cases from your experience in a business book:

- Relate the example to a specific point and be sure the match makes sense. Readers know when you're forcing a comparison between a point and an unrelated example.

- Keep your ego in check and focus on the process. If you're a consultant or sales professional, give the client credit for being forward thinking and willing to change. Portraying yourself or your company as the savior will sound like bragging.

- Throw in a case or two in which you failed to follow your own advice and paid a price for it. Showing your feet of clay will boost your believability and may endear you to the reader.

- Realize that because you were there, the case may seem more powerful to you than to the reader. Render the case vividly and give the reader enough context to understand its importance. Also, always tie off the case with a sentence or two underscoring its point.

- Avoid presenting "magical solutions" such as, "After working with us, management realized that only honest communication would improve morale." The reader wants to know *how* morale improved. How did management realize this? What did they do to communicate honestly? Rather than touting only the result, describe the process in enough (but not too much) detail.

The question always arises: Can you name names? The answer, given nondisclosure agreements, privacy rights, and the need to earn a living, is, only with permission. Permission may not be necessary if the case and the names you name are already in the public record. Discuss these situations with your editor, and get permission when necessary. If you believe it would be useful, show the passages in question to the client or customer, but don't let them water down the material or bury the lesson. In fact, don't show them material if you know they will nix it. Instead, use the case without naming them. Disguised cases usually work well, if not as well as those with real names. We've all read about "an appliance-store chain in Ohio" or "a major aerospace firm" and so on. Most readers accept these designations. Avoid coy "disguises" such as a "major software company based in Redmond, Washington." People may enjoy guessing which company you straightened out, and that's fine. But don't identify the company while "disguising" it.

Real-life cases from your own files establish you as the voice of experience in the reader's mind. It's the most powerful tool you have.

Primary research constitutes your next most powerful tool, and it is a very close second. Interviews, surveys, and studies conducted or commissioned by you or your firm are your property. You can publish them as you see fit, with due respect for the respondents' confidentiality. Primary research can even serve as the basis of the book. *The Millionaire Next Store* is an excellent example. So is Emmett Murphy's *Leadership IQ*.

However, be sure to flesh out the research results with plentiful examples, cases, and anecdotes gathered during the research. A trade book cannot present research findings the way a report would. They must be brought to life for the reader.

Secondary research produces many of the examples found in business books. The good thing about material drawn from the public press and public knowledge—its familiarity—is also a negative. On the positive side, many readers will be familiar with the case. You only have to mention the Enron scandal or Coca-Cola's global success, and everyone will know what you are talking about. You can sketch in the details you want to focus on and save the lengthy explanations.

On the negative side, certain cases, companies, and people have become clichés. Moreover, it's tempting to attribute a well-known company's success to the subject of the book, whether it is superb leadership, relentless innovation, or tireless customer service. It's equally tempting to attribute failure to the absence of the characteristic in question. Readers know that success and failure actually stem from a mix of characteristics. They forgive these facile comparisons because they realize you are just making a point, but don't presume that their mercy is infinite. When you use cases from secondary sources, dig deep. Go beyond the usual suspects. Check out the business sections of various cities' newspapers. Local companies have terrific stories that nobody outside their area has heard. You can convert this to primary research by telephoning the person who was interviewed for the article and getting more information and juicy quotes that relate directly to your point.

Secondary research has its place. Just don't ask it to carry the book. Consider it an adjunct to your own experience and primary research.

Composite cases you create include "John Smith" cases as well as composites assembled from real life. This is a gray area. Business books are nonfiction, and everything in them is supposed to be factual. Yet most editors allow examples such as: "John Smith signed a noncompete clause when he joined Acme Company as a senior engineer. Six years later, when he left to start his own business, Acme took him to court."

Would the editor and reader prefer a real example? You bet. Wouldn't you? But when you lack a real-life example, or nobody would want to be linked to a situation, or legal issues or libel laws make it impossible to use a real case study, a composite or "John Smith" case makes sense.

Use composite and anonymous cases sparingly. Avoid them when possible. Then again, Stephen Covey used first-name cases and sample conversations to illustrate points in *The Seven Habits of Highly Effective People* with no apparent loss of credibility or sales.

Create Comparisons with Similes, Analogies, and Metaphors

First, a review may be in order. A simile compares one thing to another, usually using the word "like," as in "Growing a business is like tending a garden." An analogy equates one thing to another to clarify or emphasize a point. For instance, "R&D is to a company as seed corn is to a farm." A metaphor uses a more memorable or tangible item as a stand-in for the thing being discussed. It is metaphorical to say, "A company's fields will lie fallow without vigorous R&D."

Such comparisons work well in business books because of the conceptual nature of much of the material. It's no coincidence that business people constantly employ comparisons in conversation. War and sports metaphors abound. We talk about the battle for market share, executives leading the charge, and companies picking off competitors. We speak of a level playing field, singles, home runs, touchdowns, and running interference. Certain metaphors, such as "window of opportunity," achieve wide popularity.

Metaphors work so well that many books, particularly in the 1990s, were built around metaphorical themes. These included *The Way of the Dolphin*, *The Oz Principle*, *Growing a Business*, and *Management and the New Science*. Others, such as *Swim with the Sharks without Being Eaten Alive* and *Guerrilla Marketing*, simply used metaphorical titles.

Metaphors like these make conceptual material easier to grasp. But the device can be stretched too far, and as of this writing business book editors are not enamored of "metaphor books." Heaven knows there have been enough of them, although sooner or later more of them will find their way into print. Book publishing trends wax and wane (like the moon).

When employed on a smaller scale, simile, analogy, and metaphor remain useful for enlivening writing and increasing reader engagement, especially when used creatively. For instance, in *TechnoLeverage* Mike Hruby compared a company's move from a leadership position in a mature product area to start-up mode in a new product area to the daredevil stunt of wing-walking:

> *As evident from the history of so many companies that once led their industries, taking the lead is easier than holding onto it. It might be useful to think of holding onto the lead in terms of wing-walking, the old county fair entertainment in which a man or woman steps from the wing of one light airplane to that of another. To survive, you must let go of the original position you have been hanging on to. This can be difficult—and scary. Then you must have a new position to go to, something to step onto and something to grasp. When the time is right, you must make your move. You ultimately have to take the step and make the leap.*

Freshness of imagery, that's the goal.

One other caveat: An image or figure of speech that's popular when a book is written may sound stale by the publication date. Therefore, try to use original (meaning your own) or enduring imagery.

Tell Them a Story Using Narrative Devices

The narrative devices at your disposal are exposition, description, dialogue, and action. In business how-to books, much of the writing is expository, but description, dialogue, and action can play a role in examples and cases, albeit in a limited way. In books on companies or people, they are the essential means of storytelling.

Exposition is telling, rather than showing. Expository writing explains the subject to the reader. Despite every writing instructor's dictate to show rather than tell, exposition has a legitimate place in writing. In business how-to books, it cannot be avoided.

Here is a passage of exposition from *Multipreneuring*:

> *We are now in the Information Age, the Age of the Smart Machine, the Age of the Knowledge Worker. This is not just the stuff of magazine covers. Rather, technology is driving most new opportunities in business. This is true even in manufacturing, where the day is not far off when production managers will reprogram instead of retool.*

The paragraph *explains* the environment that has prompted the need for multipreneuring as a career strategy.

Description depicts the physical details of a person, place, or thing for the reader.

Here is a passage of description from Stuart Crainer's *The 75 Greatest Management Decisions Ever Made*:

> *Forty or not, Barbie defies the aging process in a defiantly old-fashioned sort of way. No cellulite in sight, Barbie has long legs and a figure as shapely as shapely could be. Translated from doll size into reality, Barbie would stand seven feet tall with five-foot long legs. Her stats would be 40-22-36. One might have thought that the sexist freak show Barbie style would now be outdated. Not so. A Barbie doll is bought every two seconds. That's one billion and counting. Barbie…is now a $1.9 billion industry.*

This passage, which introduces a section on successful brand extension (in the form of Ken and so on), describes Barbie's bizarre physique and amazing financial attributes.

Dialogue and *action* are the most powerful narrative devices. Dialogue and action work together to create scenes. Portraying scenes is essential to narratives about companies, entrepreneurs, or executives, but even in how-to books they have a place. For instance, the following brief passage from *Big League Business Thinking* employs dialogue and action to create a picture of a man who firmly believes in reflective thinking, one of the skills taught in the book:

> *Jimmy walked across my office, sat down behind my desk, leaned back in my chair, clasped his hands behind his head, and propped his feet on top of the desk. [action] "If I am doing my job right," he said, "I am spending part of my time doing this. I am taking time out from day-to-day operations, putting my feet up, and thinking reflectively about where my business is going." [dialogue]*

A narrative nonfiction business book requires a good command of narrative techniques, as well as the journalist's research and reporting skills. If you've never written narrative nonfiction and have committed yourself to writing such a business book, read up on the subject and seek formal instruction if necessary. Take time to study the best in the genre, which include *Barbarians at the Gate: The Fall of RJR Nabisco* by Bryan Burrough and John Helyar and *Greed and Glory on Wall Street: The Fall of the House of Lehman* and *World War 3.0: Microsoft Vs. the U.S. Government, and the Battle to Rule the Digital Age* by former *New Yorker* staff writer Ken Auletta.

Quote Facts and Figures

Business people enjoy facts and figures, which is good, because facts and figures strongly support an author's points. Omit them and you may receive editorial comments such as, "Do you have evidence of this?" and "Support this statement!"

Quote sources of facts and figures. Naming your sources enhances your credibility and, more important, gives credit where it's due. Failure to do so might raise copyright issues. Even if you're not creating a work of journalism, be as accurate as possible and keep good records of your sources. Realize, too, that certain readers are skeptical of statistics and will mentally challenge them. Avoid any faulty applications of statistics, and if you have made any calculations yourself, triple-check them.

Draw a Picture for the Reader

Used properly, diagrams, charts, and illustrations can do what most of the tools in this chapter do: express concepts in ways that help readers comprehend them. Diagrams make concepts more concrete. They also help you reach readers who learn best through visual media. Even those who learn best through words will appreciate the occasional break in the text.

Diagrams and charts are best used sparingly, however. You don't want to turn your book into a hard-copy PowerPoint presentation. If you have any doubts about the number or content of diagrams, charts, or illustrations you're using, solicit your editor's opinion and proceed accordingly. It's also wise to develop diagrams as you write the text that they will accompany. That way, the words and pictures will work together and, when the writing is finished, the diagrams will be there, ready to submit with the manuscript.

What's Funny?

Humor in business books is an iffy proposition, as it is in business itself. Most people fail to see their careers, investments, organizations, or business decisions as laughing matters. Moreover, by its nature, humor tends to be irreverent and potentially offensive. Approach your subject with the mindset of a comedian and people will, naturally, fail to take you seriously. Yet a trade book should be entertaining if at all possible.

What's a business book author to do?

First, an entertaining theme for the book or sections of it can provide a reference point or a platform for droll observations or occasional wordplay. The first-rate guide to winning at office politics, *Cain and Abel at Work* by Gerry Lange and Todd Domke, and all of the "Leadership-Secrets-of..." books employ such motifs.

Second, if edgy humor keeps elbowing its way into your manuscript, let it. You may as well entertain yourself as you write the blasted thing. You can always edit it out later, or leave it for the editor to deal with. Just don't go bananas if she deletes it. And if you know for sure that something is *too* edgy, delete it yourself before you submit it. Too edgy means humor at the expense of the opposite sex or foreign, ethnic, or religious groups; it also includes political, vulgar, or marital humor. Finally, avoid self-deprecating humor unless you handle it well. It typically falls flat on the page and undercuts your authority.

Confine attempts at humor to pure corn, gentle irony, dry wit, *limited* wordplay, and humorous quotes. Irony and wit add to the pleasure of reading Thomas Stewart's writing. In *The Wealth of Knowledge*, he made the point that intellectual assets are underworked by stating that, "Most knowledge lives the life of Riley, curled up on someone's couch, asleep between sheets in someone's file cabinet, undisturbed on someone's hard drive..."

We're not trying for knee-slappers here, but quotes can contribute chuckles. Masters of illogical logic, such as Sam Goldwyn ("If people don't want to go to a movie, you can't keep them away.") and Yogi Berra ("We're lost, but we're making good time."), have uttered many gags applicable to business. Gertrude

Stein, Groucho Marx, W.C. Fields, Woody Allen, and Lily Tomlin are also likely sources.

Don't Forget Format

Finally, format can help you engage the reader in various ways. Tools of formatting include headings and subheads, bulleted or numbered lists, boxes and callouts, indenting and italics, beginning-of-chapter quotations and end-of-chapter summaries. Such devices catch and direct the reader's attention—as long as they are not overused, in which case they cause confusion.

The right format not only creates white space to provide a break for readers, it also gives browsers and skimmers entry points into the text. Many people skim or skip sections or read for highlights, and that's their right. A good format helps these customers. I had a colleague once who resisted using subheads, bullets, and summaries in his reports because, he said, he wanted to "force them to read it all." This was almost certainly counter-productive. As Sam Goldwyn may have said, "You can lead a horse to water, but you can't make him read."

Reach Around the World

Foreign language rights for an English-language business book of any merit or popularity are typically sold to overseas publishers (usually by the publisher, sometimes by the agent). Online bookstores open a worldwide market for business books in English. With English now indisputably the global business language, the potential is expanding for worldwide sales of English-language editions of business books.

This being the case, it may be useful to consider modifying or omitting American colloquialisms or cultural references that could be obscure or offensive to foreign audiences. Doing so may lead to a more coherent translation for readers in foreign-language markets. It will also provide a better read for non-native speakers of English who read the English version. (Few business books are translated into all major languages.)

On the other hand, you don't want to write bland, expressionless text. It comes down to a judgment call, based on the type of book and its market. I raise the issue here because it has arisen with publishers I've worked with. Mention it to your editor and follow her lead.

Business Book Writing Guidelines

Almost every book publisher has a document called "Author's Guidelines" or the house "Style Guide." Be sure to request this as soon as you go to contract. The guide will focus mainly on small points of the house style—whether three million dollars is written $3,000,000 or $3 million and whether to use the serial comma, that is, the comma before "and" in a series of three or more items (as in, "executives, managers, and supervisors").

However, the better style guides also discuss how formal or informal the writing style of the book should be and how to format the manuscript and submit diagrams. Most editors don't want authors to worry about tiny details like serial commas. The copy editor and proofreader will catch those later. They do want you to understand the house's overall approach to material and how to submit the manuscript and diagrams. Make sure you review the style guide and discuss any questions you have with your editor before you start to write.

Writing It Right

Here are a quick-and-dirty dozen ways to improve your writing:

1. Take a three-step approach—plan/draft/edit—and execute them as three separate steps. First plan, even if it's a rough

outline or a list of points you'll cover in a chapter or section. Then draft it, quickly, and don't edit as you draft. Then edit it into something that sings.

2. Write with nouns and verbs. Minimize the use of adjectives and adverbs.

3. Avoid the verb "to be" in all its forms. It's the weakest verb in the English language. It indicates mere existence. Very often we're stuck with it, but find a stronger word whenever possible.

4. Read your writing aloud. If it sounds clanky, rewrite it. If you're out of breath by the time you get to the end of a sentence, edit it down.

5. Edit sentences by deleting every needless word and breaking long sentences into two or three sentences.

6. Keep a good dictionary and thesaurus handy, and use them.

7. Read, especially the kinds of books that you want to write.

8. If you write elaborate or emotional "purple prose" be aware of it and heed editors' suggestions, but don't despair. On the scale of authorial evils, this sin ranks fairly low. At least you have some passion, and editors can work with that kind of writer. As the saying goes, it's easier to tame a tiger than puff up a pussycat.

9. Feel free to overwrite at the drafting stage, and then fix it in the editing stage. Overwriting here refers to both purple

prose and too much text. If you are a word factory, you probably write fast. So write fast and fix it later.

10. Even in a how-to book, adhere to journalistic practices as much as possible. You may not be pursuing a Pulitzer, but solid facts, credible sources, and orderly notes can only improve the writing and the book.

11. Remember, you are writing a business book, not *Paradise Lost*. If good is the enemy of great, perfectionism is the enemy of completion.

12. When dealing with an editor, keep control-freak tendencies in check. Don't agree to anything abhorrent, but know that writing a business book is a collaborative process. Request feedback and listen to it. Often you'll find that suggestions you initially disagree with actually improve the book, or at least don't harm it.

Keep the Faith

Writing can be a joy or a slog. Most books offer ample opportunity to experience both. Belief in the material and in the value of the book, along with sheer persistence, will take you a long way. On any book project you will, out of necessity, develop and practice new skills and learn new things, and that never hurt anyone.

In that same vein, you will also have to recognize, analyze, and solve problems as they arise in the publishing process. The next chapter will help you do that.

The Manuscript Is Finished, But the Project Isn't

Working Well with Your Publisher and Troubleshooting Problems

 ompleting the manuscript stands as a significant milestone. However, more than half of the work of creating a successful book still lies ahead. Most of that will consist of marketing and promotion, the subject of the next chapter. This chapter covers the remaining tasks necessary to produce a finished book. It also shows how to address problems that arise in writing, publishing, and collaborating on a book.

The Editing and Production Process

If your editor reviews the manuscript and says that it needs only a light copy edit, she may be right or she may be wrong. If your project is on a tight deadline and resources are limited, the editor may judge the book to be "good enough" and allocate the resources to another manuscript. It's frustrating, but that other manuscript may get a careful edit because it was not as well written as yours. If your manuscript receives a meticulous edit, be thankful. Unless the editor totally rewrites it or calls in a book doctor, it doesn't mean that it is badly written. It means that you're getting valuable input that will improve your book.

A Bit about Editing

Broadly, there are two types of editing in book publishing—developmental editing and copy editing, also known as line editing.

Some acquisition editors take a strong role in developing a book, while others hand it off to a separate developmental editor. On the other hand, many publishers don't provide much developmental editing, and that's a shame. Developmental editing improves the book's structure, approach, and coverage of the material. Working from the proposal, the developmental editor can do much of this before the actual writing begins, although it also occurs after a draft of the manuscript is in hand. Developmental editors recommend deleting, adding, combining or changing the order of chapters or sections of chapters. They suggest points to cover in various chapters and sources for additional material. They can "talk story" with an author writing a narrative of a company or an executive. They develop new chapter titles, ideas for leads in chapters and sections, and other ways of making the book more accurate, complete, and exciting.

A copy editor works on the completed manuscript to improve the quality, accuracy, and style of the book. Copy editors delete repetitive or unnecessary material. They ask authors to support or expand certain statements. They streamline sentences, improve word choice, and correct grammar, punctuation, and usage errors. They conform the text to the house style (a task they share with the proofreader).

In addition, the editorial team will occasionally have the manuscript reviewed by an expert on the subject other than the author. This person, often an academic or another author who has written on the subject, verifies facts and provides a "second opinion" on the material.

Every author needs editors, proofreaders, and fact-checkers. Every year they save thousands of writers and millions of readers from bad experiences.

Wonderful, you're thinking, this sounds like genuine value added. Please hold that thought when an editor provides four pages of single-spaced comments on a proposed book or marks your manuscript up to a fare-thee-well. Although editorial comments are valuable, a high volume of them can leave an author overwhelmed. New writers in particular see heavily marked-up pages as a stinging rebuke or an insurmountable workload. Actually, when handled correctly, even heavy criticism is constructive and manageable.

Handling Editorial Comments

Editors do tend to be critical. It's part of their job. Few of them have "bolster writers' egos" on their to-do lists. At times editorial comments may seem abrupt or even harsh. However, editors are not out to destroy writers. Those who wield a sharp pencil know what they're doing and have the readers' best interests at heart. They expect authors to be professional and a bit thick-skinned. Regardless of the amount or tone of the comments, the criticism is meant to be constructive.

Take editorial comments in that spirit. There's no sense in being "word proud" or falling in love with a particular passage. Editing and editorial comments invariably improve a piece. This doesn't mean that every single correction and comment improves the piece. But the overall effort definitely does.

Editorial comments do increase an author's workload. Yet the work necessary to address editorial comments almost always turns out to be far less than the author thought it would be on first viewing the marked-up copy.

If you are a new or sensitive author, when an editor returns heavily marked-up material, skim it to get the gist of the comments and then set it aside for a day or two. Give any feelings of resentment or disappointment time to subside before returning to it. Then evaluate each change and comment one by one. (For our purposes, a change alters the text, while a comment requests or suggests change, clarification, more information, or other action on the part of the author.) Taken individually, most editorial changes and comments fall into one of the following categories:

1. Changes to the text that improve it
2. Changes that don't improve the text, but don't harm it
3. Changes that change the meaning or otherwise harm the text
4. Comments that can be ignored or easily addressed
5. Comments that can be addressed with difficulty

If you simply accept editorial changes of the first and second type, you will move things along and generate goodwill. Try to repair changes of the third type in ways that the editor will accept. Where that's not possible, discuss the changes with the editor.

A surprising number of editorial comments—those in the fourth category above—can be easily addressed by consulting a print or Web-based resource, making a phone call, or adding a bit more of your own knowledge. Comments that are either off the mark (because the editor doesn't know the subject as well as the author) or that are clearly just suggestions ("It would be nice to…" or "Is there any chance we could…") can often be ignored, unless addressing them would add enough value. Editors realize that some of their suggestions will be off the mark—either impractical or nice but not necessary.

Valid comments that can be addressed with difficulty—the fifth category above—require the most attention and often some negotiation. Editors rarely put forth make-work suggestions. Some ideas demand more work than they are worth, but others require significant work that would repay itself. If the editor tells you that your book should definitely cover something not covered or that a chapter needs to be expanded or restructured, seriously consider it. Discuss her reasoning. Perhaps a legislative change, economic development, or other event has changed the landscape during the writing of the book. Perhaps a just-published competitive book covers material that your book omits but should also cover. Consider easy fixes that could do the job. (Also consider the question: "Is it worth pushing back the publication date to include this material?") Ultimately, the decision to spend more time and resources on the book should be based on the costs versus the benefits.

If a developmental or copy editor insists that you try it his way, do so. You will either find that the suggestion works or discover a great reason for not implementing it. After all, if you try it and can't make it work, then you have done your best.

Finally, differences of opinion can often be settled by simply deleting the troublesome passage. It won't work every time but when it does, it works really well.

After the copy edit, the manuscript should be accurate, complete, and free of all but small errors, which will be fixed by the proofreader. Communicate regularly with your editor to ensure that you know when the book is going to layout (the process that converts manuscript pages to book pages) because it is difficult and expensive to make changes to the book after the pages are laid out.

Going into Production

Definitions of when a book "goes into production" vary slightly among publishers. At most houses, it means that the manuscript has been accepted by the editor and sent on to copy editing, proofreading, and page and cover design. These steps are all necessary before printing, binding, packing, and shipping of the book. (At fast-moving houses, page and cover design begins when the first third or half of the manuscript has been delivered.)

When the manuscript goes to page design, a designer chooses a typeface and lays out the pages in a desktop publishing system. Authors have little or no control over this process. While there are better and worse layouts, page design occurs without a major mishap on most business books.

Again—and your editor will stress this—few changes can be made to the book after the pages have been laid out in final form. Page proofs, which are copies of the pages as they will appear in the book, are sent to the author for review. By then editors expect few changes and no major ones. The author will usually have two chances to review and edit the page proofs. After the author's first round of edits to the proofs, most publishers charge the author for further changes other than those needed to fix typographical errors. (By this point in the process, the publisher's editorial staff should have caught all typos.) These further, non-typo-related changes, known as AA's (for "authors alterations") are not encouraged. However, minor, necessary ones are permitted and charged to the author, at a reasonable rate, against the remaining unpaid advance or the royalties.

Diagrams, a staple of business how-to books, require special attention at this point. Errors in diagrams are easy to miss. Also, diagrams often appear quite different in page proofs than on manuscript pages. Make sure charts are properly laid out and correctly labeled. Ask the editor or page designer to ensure that the legends and labels in all diagrams will be readable and that light or dark shading will show up properly in the final product.

Get the Index in

As noted in Chapter 3, the contract should stipulate that the book will have an index. If, because of a budget or schedule crunch, the editor decides not to do an index after all, politely insist that your book have one. Gently point out that the contract calls for one, if that's the case (which it should be), and that you believe that it will help sell the book.

If necessary, hire an indexer yourself. Or, if you have the time and patience, read the manuscript, make a list of indexable terms, and use the "Find" command in your word-processing program to locate the words. You will still have to search the page proofs for every term because the page numbers in the manuscript will not match those in the final book. Tedious, but probably worth it, if, for whatever reason, you can't hire an indexer.

Judging Books' Covers

Most professional authors have a sad story or two about book covers, and I'm no exception. Still, there are happy stories as well. Once, when a book I worked on wound up with a beautiful cover, I called my agent to share the joy. He had already seen it and agreed that it was beautiful. Then he said, "Their regular designers must have been out sick that week."

Authors often feel their covers misrepresent their books, confuse potential purchasers, or otherwise undermine the product. Almost as often, they are at least partly correct. The root of the problem is no mystery: The designer has not read the book. This doesn't mean that all book covers will be botched. But it increases the proportion of botched covers. Designers are not paid to read the books, and they are far too busy to volunteer. Nor do they usually ask authors about their books, let alone their ideas for the jacket design. Meanwhile, editors, who have larger problems to cope with, tend to profess enthusiasm for whatever the designers design.

How can authors improve their chances of getting a well-designed cover?

First, in early discussions of the publication schedule, ask the editor when the cover will be designed. As that date approaches, express real interest in the cover. Mention the best one or two ideas you have for the design. As a damage control measure, it may be worth suggesting a simple, perhaps minimalist, cover, if that style would work for the book.

Second, if, when you see the cover design, you feel it has been botched, don't respond immediately. Instead, figure out what's wrong with it. Be sure to look beyond matters of taste. Then write a memo that stresses your belief that the cover is a key element in marketing the book, which it is. Identify one or two features of the cover that work, and then the features that you believe will negatively affect potential buyers. The latter might include unclear, confusing, or ambiguous images or typefaces, murky or otherwise "off" colors, and derivative or off-putting photos, artwork, or graphics. Show the cover to other people and get their comments. Doing so will give you a few ideas while helping you regain perspective because, inevitably, one or two people will like it. Revise the memo accordingly.

Finally, you or your agent—whoever has more willingness, clout, and diplomacy—should fax, e-mail, or mail the memo to the editor and talk the issue over with her on the phone. (Be aware that your agent may disagree about the cover or simply not want to hassle the editor over it.) Don't expect miracles. Without massive leverage, the chances of getting a whole new cover are close to nil. Once design resources have been invested in a cover, most publishers refuse requests to increase their investment. Besides, the second cover might not work any better, in which case you'd either have to settle for it, perhaps with minor changes, or risk being labeled "difficult." But do make your case regarding the initial cover. With sound reasoning and respect for all involved, it is possible to have the most egregious features of a bad dust jacket changed.

Jacket Blurbs

On the subject of the dust jacket, at some point your editor will ask you for names of famous people who might supply brief testimonials, known as blurbs, for the back cover. Blurbs catch readers' attention and help sell the book. Ah, but what if you don't know anyone famous? Or what if the celebrities you know have nothing to do with the topic of the book?

All is not lost. Plumb your personal digital assistant or Rolodex for anyone who a) has any measure of business fame, b) might know someone who might supply a blurb, or c) heads, or even works in, a major company or other famous organization.

Think about your dentist, your lawyer, your accountant, your architect. Who do they know? Comb through your clients and suppliers. Throw the search open. Call in IOUs. Asking for a blurb is asking for a favor. Many people can't be bothered. However, others are flattered or at least like the idea of getting their name on a book they didn't even have to read. (Offer a synopsis of the book, a few chapters of the manuscript or, if available, page proofs or a bound galley. They can read whatever they want.)

Then you can always ask famous people who don't know you. If the topic is dear to their hearts and your cover letter sings, you may get lucky. Famous people all had help becoming famous, and some pay back their benefactors (on a cosmic level) by doing the same for someone else—maybe someone like you.

Allow time for the blurb-search. That means starting long before the editor requests them, which tends to be just as the cover is going into design. It takes time to find people willing to supply blurbs, and approaching them on a rush basis is bad form.

Finally, ask your editor if she knows anyone. Most editors

know famous people, or at least authors with name recognition. In fact, considering how many authors write blurbs for each other's books in apparent *quid pro quo*, one might reasonably assume that editors would be the market makers in these transactions. If that's the case, the market is not a very open one, and most editors tend to be less than forthcoming. It can't hurt to ask though.

Although blurbs help, a book without them is not doomed. The absence of blurbs has the virtue of freeing up space on the back cover for additional marketing copy.

Housekeeping Issues

A well-published book is the result of hundreds of small things done correctly. Yet some small things can get lost amid the larger issues involved in expressing ideas in book form. Given this reality, here are a few things to keep in mind while writing the manuscript and seeing it through the editing and production process:

- Understand the means by which the editor wants the manuscript submitted. Many now want only e-mail attachments or a disk.
- Be equally clear about the format for submitting diagrams. Some houses want a disk, while others want line drawings for their illustrators to reproduce in a form they can use.
- Keep good records, label your files and interview tapes, and take care of other organizational details *as you go along*.
- Secure written permission to use any material that requires it. Talk to your editor about this. Request written permission early, and be ready to submit the required documentation to your editor soon after you submit the manuscript.
- Keep track of promises you make to send your interview subjects (and anyone else) a copy of the book. When it's published, send them a signed copy.
- Have a flattering photo of yourself readily available for the

inside back-cover flap. Editors invariably request this picture as the cover is going to press, sending the author on a frantic search through photo albums or on a mad dash to a photographer. Plan ahead.

All of the foregoing notwithstanding, there's still that old saying: If you want to make God laugh, tell Him your plans. That and Murphy's Law are the reasons for the next section.

When the Going Gets Tough
Some problems in the writing and publishing process are predictable, but they are few. What is predictable is that there will be problems.

Writerly Worries
Most writers and business people are familiar with the six phases of a project, defined by a gifted but anonymous business thinker:
1. Enthusiasm
2. Panic
3. Despair
4. Search for the guilty
5. Punishment of the innocent
6. Rewards for bystanders

These, of course, apply to writing a business book just as they apply to any other lengthy project involving various professionals. Landing a book contract ignites a burst of enthusiasm, quickly followed by panic—a feeling familiar to anyone who has sold a project they've never done before.

Many authors experience despair on every book, even if it's their fifth, six, or seventh. Often the feeling descends when, even after the adrenaline administered by panic, they still don't know how they're ever going to fill 250 pages with something people will pay to read. Even seasoned authors entertain the idea of wiggling out of a contract, returning the money, and getting honest work at a resume-writing service.

Other authors manage to fend off despair until the dreaded "middle passage," which would be chapters five through eight in a ten-chapter book. These chapters resemble the fabled horse latitudes, that belt of dead air that sailors of old encountered between the trade winds (the first few chapters) and the westerlies (the final two). The antidote to despair—and the phase of a project that's missing from our six-phase scheme—is simple but difficult: Keep working. It's the only way to finish the book. As the saying goes, writing is the art of applying the seat of the pants to the seat of the chair. Only actual, productive time spent getting the words down on paper will produce a book.

The final three phases of a project occur if, and only if, the book fails to sell and the returns stack up in the warehouses. In such cases, the identities of the guilty, the innocent, and the bystanders depend on the project and on the magnitude of the debacle.

Trouble-Shooting Writing and Publishing Problems

Normal problems of the day-to-day, take-it-in-stride variety crop up in research, writing, and publication, as they do any process. The following problems, however, can befoul not only the book but also relationships and even the reputations of the people involved:

- Short deadlines
- Missed delivery dates
- Editorial turnover
- Professional writers who don't deliver
- Expert-authors who lack material
- Slow paying or nonpaying clients

Short Deadlines

An unreasonably short deadline generally hurts a book. Unless the book is highly formulaic, "unreasonably short" means three to five months or less. Although books have been written in two weeks, they were either bad books or books by geniuses. Short deadlines arise when business concerns overwhelm quality considerations. It's happened to me, and it was a bad experience. It wasn't the hard work and long hours that hurt. Indeed, such projects can be quite profitable because the advance or fee is earned over a shorter elapsed time. It's the damage to the book that hurts.

As with most large problems, prevention beats repair. Chapter 3 noted ways of avoiding short deadlines, but occasionally, despite the author's protests, an editor insists on an early delivery date. Professional writers want to be seen as people who can deliver. They don't want to "disappoint" an editor, even if the deadline is unreasonable. As an author, you can simply refuse to deliver on the desired date and cite quality or scheduling as the reason. But will that editor want to do business with you again? Keep in mind the legitimate reasons for short deadlines, such as a competitive book in the pipeline at another publisher.

When a short deadline cannot be avoided:

- Spend a day or two revising the project plan, if one was already in place. Create an accelerated plan geared to meeting the new deadline.

- Minimize the need for research of any kind. Do away with any expendable sections of the book that require it.

- For any necessary research, hire a research assistant or one of the outfits that offers writers that kind of support (usually at premium rates). Provide very specific instructions about the facts, figures, examples, cases, or quotes you need.

- Use all of your (and your agent's) persuasive powers to get maximum editorial support from the publisher. Warn the editor that you may be submitting ragged drafts on some chapters or sections, but do so only on material that the copy editor can readily slap into shape.

- If the project is a collaboration, the expert-author and ghostwriter must sit down for several days, totally undisturbed, to capture material on audiotape for each chapter. Send the tapes to a transcription service immediately and pay their rush-service rates, if necessary.

- Tell your family, friends, and clients that you are going under for the duration of the writing of the manuscript. Then do exactly that and write like mad. Writing partners must move material between them quickly, on an agreed-upon schedule.

- Don't agree to submit the manuscript to the editor one chapter at a time. It gets too hectic and reduces opportunities to switch text around in the manuscript. Submit it in halves, thirds, or three-chapter chunks.

Most professional writers, regardless of the genre in which they work, have the sensibilities of craftspeople. It pains them to submit work that they know isn't their best. The realities of publishing, however, sometimes dictate that they do their best quickly.

Missed Delivery Dates

Occasionally authors do miss even reasonable manuscript delivery dates. An editor told me of a case in which the book was included in the fall sales catalog and orders had been taken, but the book would not be ready until the following season—at best. When asked if this were unusual, he replied, "Not unusual enough."

If you realize you're going to miss a submission deadline—reasonable or not—for a section of the manuscript, it's time to redo the project plan. It's also time to notify the editor. Tell her honestly when she can expect which portions of the book. Don't err on the side of optimism or you'll miss two deadlines rather than one. Listen to any suggestions she has for speeding things up, and use them if you can. It also won't hurt to apologize. After all, she looks bad to her colleagues, and her boss may be questioning her project management skills.

Do everything possible to stick to the revised deadline. Also, review the previous section, Short Deadlines, for ideas on how to work quickly.

Editorial Turnover

A book usually suffers when its acquiring editor leaves the publisher, taking her sponsorship with her. This is probably less of a problem at a smaller house; at a large house, the book often becomes an orphan. It's the downside of having the acquiring editor "own" the project: When she leaves, no one owns it.

When an editor leaves, her books are assigned to another editor. That editor may lack interest in the project. Of course, from a business standpoint the new editor *should* make the best go of any book he's handed. The book represents a potentially valuable asset to the publisher. Given this, it should be nurtured, launched, and supported as vigorously by the new editor as it would have been by the acquiring editor.

But think about it: You're in a company in a staff position doing some kind of project-based work. A colleague leaves the company and her projects are divided among the remaining staff. Would you put the same effort into the departed colleague's projects as you put into your own? Probably not. Organizational life being what it is, you'd give priority to your own projects. The decision to acquire a book, moreover, is one that involves large measures of taste, intuition, and forecasts of the future, all of which differ markedly from one person to another. Editors either bond or don't bond with certain books.

As your editor leaves, wish her well and find out where she's headed and how to stay in touch, particularly if she's moving to another publisher. If you haven't already learned the names of the other people working on your book—the copy editor, production editor, and publicity person—get them from the departing editor, along with the name of the editor-in-chief or whomever the editor reported to. Phone or e-mail these people to introduce or reintroduce yourself and to say that you look forward to working with them to see the book through the remainder of the process.

As soon as you learn the name of your new editor, get in touch. Update him on the project and if practical ask to get together for lunch, drinks, or dinner, or at his office. Develop a relationship with the new editor. Emphasize that you will do everything you can to make the book successful. Then redouble your efforts to promote and sell the book, even if you feel you are already fully committed. Your added support must compensate for any loss of support on the publisher's end.

Turnover plagues book publishing because of relatively low pay, continual mergers and acquisitions, periodic cut-backs, and mobile employees. The books, and by extension their authors, take the worst hit. It's a blow that must be absorbed, and it can be, if the author takes nothing for granted.

Professional Writers Who Don't Deliver

Suppose you are a business person—an expert-author—and you've hired a professional writer to ghost a book, but for whatever reason he cannot write the manuscript. (If you have hired him to write the proposal and he cannot deliver, you still have a problem, but you don't have the pressure of having to deliver a book under contract.) The writer may have met with an accident or developed personal or health problems. Or, after the glow of landing the book contract wore off, you and he may have discovered irreconcilable creative or personality differences.

The earlier this problem is diagnosed, the better. If it's not addressed quickly, missed deadlines lay ahead. When a writer cannot deliver, you need a new one—fast.

Here's how to proceed:

- If the writer's drafts are delayed past your agreed deadline with the writer (let alone with the editor), you must learn why. If his other commitments are the problem, either he must get them out of the way or you must drop him. If his inability to deal with the material is the problem, further working sessions regarding the proposal or the book are in order.

- If the quality of the writer's material is poor, document the problems objectively. Analyze the content and style and list the shortcomings. If you're not sure of your judgment, show the material to someone whose literary taste can be trusted and ask her what's wrong with it. Take notes. You need to meet with the writer and give him specific, constructive criticism.

- When you meet with the writer, set a deadline—say, a week or two—for getting the project back on track. If you don't see good text by then, you need to replace him. Be candid about this and adhere to the terms of your contract with him.

- When you talk to the editor, try to present the solution along with the problem. If you can't quickly replace the writer, tell the editor. You may need an extension on the manuscript delivery date, and the editor has a right to know this as soon as possible.

- Have the proposal and all relevant materials organized for prospective writers to review. Also, continue to compile material that you know the new writer will need and be sure to obtain all material developed by the departing writer.

For whatever reason—trust, optimism, or blindness—expert-authors often act too slowly in addressing this problem. It's better to pay attention to any doubts you have and be ready to face the facts, if necessary. If the writer needs to be replaced and you have an agent on the project, ask her for names of other business book writers. The editor may be able to recommend a writer, and you should check out Web sites that list writers or allow you to post a project. The issue will be timing. Good writers tend to be busy, though they can often shift things around to accommodate a rush job. Do what you would do in any situation when someone drops the ball on a project—move quickly to hire someone who can do the job.

Expert-Authors Who Lack Material

Let's reverse the situation in the previous section. Suppose you are a professional writer with a book under contract and the expert-author cannot deliver useful material. If he or his company simply pulls out of the project, it's Game Over: The book is scratched, and you move on to your next project. That's unfortunate, but an even thornier problem arises when an expert-author wants to do the book but turns out to be light on material, ideas, experiences, war stories, and case histories. The reasons for this include authors with great platforms for selling books (for instance, fame) but meager content, and authors with theoretical knowledge but few real-life cases to support their theories. Sometimes a ghost-writer hired to write a book proposal discovers during the writing of the book that he oversold his client in the proposal.

In such situations you could simply leave the project. In practice, most professional writers with a book contract and a client in hand prefer to wring whatever material they can from the author and write the book anyway. Here are ways of conducting this painful process:

- Mine the expert-author's written material deeply for every available nugget. Ask for more material. Demand to see more stuff, even if the author thinks it's irrelevant.

- Interview the author intensively. Ask penetrating questions and follow-ups, allow lengthy pauses for him to fill, and probe for concrete examples and details. When examples come up, ask who, what, when, where, why, and how. If he has no examples, ask him for hypothetical situations that show his ideas in action. Or pose them to him.

- Launch a serious secondary research effort. Put a research assistant on the project if that would help. (This person can be from the author's shop, or at least paid by the author.) In other words, if the author lacks material that shows his ideas in action, find it in the press.

- Interview other people at the author's company. If the

author denies access, tell him frankly that without it you won't have a publishable book. Network within the firm to find mavericks and junior people who'll supply straight answers and usable stories. Request access to customers, suppliers, strategic allies, investors, former employees—anyone who might have insights or stories to offer.

■ Consider recasting the book in less ambitious terms. If the expert-author's reach exceeds his grasp, delete or devote less text to the topics he can't handle and expand those he can. Also consider writing a shorter book or one in a smaller format. If that's a possibility, pitch the idea to the editor. She may take a dim view of this, so leave the door open for writing the book more or less as originally conceived.

Although the process of mining material may be painful, it can also be fruitful. Most experts who come up short on material know more than they think they know. It then becomes the writer's job to find that knowledge, supplement it with other sources, and shape it to fit the book.

Slow Paying or Nonpaying Clients

Finally, suppose you are a professional writer and you find that your client (the expert-author) cannot pay you as agreed. The situation is a potential disaster. It's one thing to be stiffed for a few hundred bucks on an article written for a fly-by-night periodical. On a book project, however, tens of thousands of dollars may be at stake.

By way of prevention, check out the creditworthiness of the author and his firm before taking the job. Avoid anyone with a history of not paying their bills. To minimize your exposure, take an initial deposit before you even start to write the proposal, another payment before starting the manuscript, and regular progress payments during the writing. At the first instance of late payment, telephone a week or so after the due date and politely follow up. If the client says he can't pay as agreed, advise him that you cannot work on that basis. Do not accept promises of payment that extend out to dates by which you will have completed most of the manuscript. If you must, ask what amount he can pay you *in the immediate future*. Whatever that number is, tell him you must think things over and get off the phone.

You could drop the project. It won't help your reputation with your editor or agent, but if you won't be paid, then drop it you must. Alternatively, you could delay the project—stop working on it until the client pays as agreed. Such a move might alienate your editor, however, who may interpret it as making your problem her problem, particularly if her publisher sees the project as a "big book." It's not your editor's fault that your client's a slow- or no-payer. Although no one expects anyone to work for free, there is a contract with the publisher to deliver a completed manuscript.

Ultimately, if you don't drop the project, you must work out a plan in which the client regularly pays you the largest possible percentage of what he owes you *and legally assigns to you*, in writing, future payments from the publisher until you are paid in full. Involve your attorney if necessary.

Accept no agreement that ends the author's obligation to pay you in full. In other words, don't agree to accept payments out of the advance and royalties that do not add up to your full fee, in lieu of your fee. Also, do not accept assurances that your client will pay you when he gets the check from the publisher. If the author is under financial pressure, paying you will not be among his priorities. Have your agent notify the publisher that all future payments should be sent to his agency until further notice, unless that is already the arrangement. Have your agent follow up to ensure that the publisher's accounting department received this message.

The Birth of a Book

The book publishing process is messier than most business people imagine. In addition to the budgets, schedules, and personalities involved in any project, publishing hinges on expression of ideas, collaboration among creative people, and matters of taste. Despite the challenges, book publishing generates a unique and particularly satisfying result—a book. It is always a thrill to see your thoughts and words on paper, between covers. As with childbirth, holding the finished product compensates for whatever hassles and heartaches occurred after conception, through gestation, and during labor.

The childbirth metaphor is apt, because the newborn book can't make its way in the world unless it is well-supported and pushed to do its best. The final chapter examines ways to give your literary offspring the support and push it needs in order to succeed.

8

Tell the World about Your Book and Your Business

Planning and Implementing a Promotion Program

Publishers believe that the author, even a midlist author, is best positioned to promote her book. That's a valid belief. After all, the author may well be the only person, aside from the copy editor and proofreader, who has actually read the thing. Moreover, a book is a unique product whose success depends on its concept, content, and value. No one can do a better job of presenting these elements to the public than the author. The author also brings genuine enthusiasm, even missionary zeal, to the task of promotion.

A staff publicist at a large publisher handles seven to twelve titles at a time. Under the circumstances, he must deploy standard communications to a standard media list. An author, on the other hand, has one book to promote, superior knowledge of the target audience, and the motivation to shape and execute a tailored publicity program. An author has more at stake in her book than any publicist and believe it or not can usually do a better job of getting it out there. But doing that job does require a plan and a commitment of time, energy, and money.

The Promotion Plan

The plan for launching a book resembles that for any other product. It uses a mix of marketing tactics to build awareness among target customers and motivate them to buy. Business book authors, particularly expert-authors, understand marketing and promotion, but they often fail to act on that understanding. Typically that's because they believe that the publisher, like most purveyors of products, will market and promote their wares.

It's more realistic to think of the publisher as the manufacturer and distributor and to think of yourself as the marketing department. The staff publicist may or may not develop a plan for the book, which he may or may not implement. Therefore, you must develop and implement a plan. Never rely on a publisher to do what every publisher openly states every author must do: be the most energetic salesperson for the book. In practice, this means putting as much into promoting the book as it took to write it and sell it to a publisher.

This chapter first examines the elements in the marketing mix as they relate to promoting business books, then looks at budgeting and scheduling. Later, it touches on ways an expert-author can use a book to build her business.

The Marketing Mix and Tricks

A good promotion plan employs several marketing tactics at once, rather than one or two. That way, the tactics support and reinforce one another. The specific marketing mix depends on the available resources and each tactic's effectiveness for a particular title.

The elements in the marketing mix include:

- Blads and bound galleys
- Review copies and other free copies of the book
- Query letters to newspapers, magazines, and newsletters
- Pitch letters to radio and television producers
- Press kit
- Advertising
- Postcards, flyers, and other direct mail
- Speaking engagements
- Book parties and a book tour
- Web-based activities
- Product extensions and other tactics

Most of these tactics work to some degree for most nonfiction genres. Yet they require special deployment to work well for business books.

Blads and Bound Galleys

Blads or bound galleys are mock-ups that show what the finished book will look like. (See Glossary.) If your publisher prepares such mock-ups, you'll receive some—talk with your editor about the number you need—to use in your promotion efforts. Blads and bound galleys help buyers for bookstores and editors at periodicals to envision the book more clearly. (Often buyers for bookstores see only the book's cover or a picture of the cover.)

Put blads or bound galleys to good use. Send them with pitch letters to targeted radio or television producers, editors at business magazines, and business-section editors at newspapers. They can also help you secure speaking engagements before business audiences.

Review Copies and Other Copies

Review copies are copies of the book sent to reviewers by the publisher. Here "other copies" means books purchased by you at the author's discount for distribution in your own promotion efforts, which might include sending books to reviewers, magazine editors, and radio and television producers, as well as for distribution to clients and prospects.

Business books are not usually reviewed by traditional book reviewers, who focus on general fiction and nonfiction. (Other genres, such as romance, sci-fi, diet, and spiritual, have the same problem.) However, you or the staff publicist should send review copies to the business magazines, newspapers, and newsletters that review business books. If the staff publicist is going to send these copies out to your list as well as to the house's list, be sure that your list includes the reviewer's or book-review editor's name. In all your PR efforts, always send the material to a specific individual.

Copies of the book should also be sent to feature editors and broadcast producers along with query and pitch letters (see below) prompting them to build stories around the theme of the book and to include the author as a interview source.

The key here is targeting. Indiscriminately sending free copies, purchased at the author's discount, to journalists, executives, and other "influential" people is a relatively low-return activity. It's possible that a Fortune 500 CEO might go gaga and order a copy for every one of his managers. But it's best to send the book only to people you have targeted as likely to have real interest in it.

Query Letters to Publications

Letters to newspapers, magazines, and newsletters should pitch the editor an exciting story angle or idea for an article that you will write or serve as a source on. The more tightly you can tie your book to a current event or other topic of media interest, the better. But even if you can't realistically make that tie, editors always need

Sample Query Letter

Dear Mr. Jones:

From a financial standpoint, most people running a small business have simply replaced their jobs. They own a business, but make the same money they did when they worked for someone else. They want more than salary replacement—but they don't know how to go about building a "real business."

Some entrepreneurs do know how. Deane Coady's home-based candy kitchen took five years to reach $200,000 in sales. After paying for ingredients, packaging, distribution, and an assistant, she netted about $43,000 annually, pre-tax. But four years later she was doing $1.3 million in sales and netting $250,000 annually, having grown into a true regional company.

Ms. Coady broke through with creative distribution strategies. For instance, she adapted one strategy from Great Bear Spring Water, examining her delivery route for *every* possible entity that might buy her products. This led to accounts she would never have considered—schools, flower shops, even police stations.

I believe readers of *Entrepreneurial Opportunities* will find the story of Coady's Candy Kitchens useful and fascinating. The attached outline shows the approach I would take to writing this 1,800 word article. I could have it on your desk four weeks after getting a green light.

Deane Coady's story is just one of those showcased in *The Million Dollar Mark: Sixteen Breakthrough Strategies for Your Small Business.* I've enclosed a complimentary copy of the book. Please consider reviewing it and looking to it for ideas for other articles (which I could write or serve as a source on).

Thank you for your consideration.

Sincerely,

John Q. Author

good ideas. Large publications have large staffs and therefore less need than smaller publications do for ideas and articles from free-lances. Yet a well-crafted letter directed to a specific editor often prompts interest, even from a large publication.

The sample query letter I present here works because:

- It is addressed to a specific individual at a publication that should have an interest in the subject of the book.
- The first paragraph presents a problem that many small entrepreneurs face: how to grow their business into a "real business."
- The second and third paragraphs provide a brief but detailed example of an entrepreneur who solved this problem, complete with numbers and a specific strategy. (Vague statements about the value of your article or book will not generate responses.)
- The fourth paragraph mentions the readers of the periodical—the audience that the editor must please. It also mentions the length of the article, which the editor may change if he wants the piece, and a timeframe for delivery.
- Finally, the last paragraph mentions the enclosed complimentary copy of the book, requests a review, and asks the editor to comb it for other article ideas (in case the one pitched in the letter fails to excite or too closely resembles another recent article in the publication).

Public relations firms follow up written pitches with a phone call. Not all editors want calls, but it's worth following up a week or so after they receive the letter. After all, as an author, you are a proven writer. You will usually reach their voice mail, so have a fifteen-second pitch ready, deliver it clearly, and leave your name and phone number at the beginning and end of the message.

Carefully target periodicals and prioritize them into A, B, and C levels by useful criteria. The most useful is the match between the book's target audience and the readership of the periodical. Other criteria include the size and range of circulation and the likelihood of a positive response from the editor. Don't focus just on big-name publications. A small magazine that directly targets your audience will often work better than a national general-interest magazine.

Reprints are a major benefit of publishing an article, even in a little-known periodical. Order reprints of the article, or get permission to reprint it, from the periodical's publisher. Then send the reprints with a cover letter to your clients, prospects, and potential readers. In the cover letter, say, "In case you missed the article I recently wrote [or, was quoted in] for *Fast Company*, here is a reprint. I believe you'll be particularly interested in...."

Efforts to place articles and obtain interviews belong in the promotion plan for any business book.

Pitch Letters to Radio and Television Producers

While radio and television may seem "glamorous," there's no reprint value. If people missed the broadcast, they missed it. (Sending out a videotape would be a bit much.) However, broadcast and cable media appearances do reach some viewers and represent good credits for you as a speaker.

They may even sell books. Although radio often taps the wrong audience for business book authors, National Public Radio is a pipeline to upscale, educated individuals who buy books. NPR's *The Connection*, produced out of Boston, often covers business, management, financial, and technology topics. *Marketplace*, produced out of Los Angeles, represents another excellent venue on NPR. Similarly, cable television's *Power Lunch* on CNBC occasionally features business book authors. Also check out local business news and feature programming in your area.

A pitch letter to a show's producer resembles one for an editor. Instead of offering an article, give them story ideas and offer to provide input and to serve as an interview subject. The more newsworthy the story idea, the better. If possible, try to link your book to a trend or event already in the news.

You may get to appear solo, or the producer might decide that two or three panelists would work better. By the way, if you will appear frequently on radio or television, hire a professional coach to assess and improve your on-air communication skills. Virtually every high-profile person who appears repeatedly in the media has had that training.

Press Kit

A press kit pulls material on the book and author together in one folder for distribution to the print and broadcast media and conference producers. Essential elements include press releases, background on and a photograph of the author, and contact information for the author or publicist. The kit can also include (positive) reviews of the book, reprints of articles by the author, and items of promotional value.

The cost of a press kit depends on the type and amount of material included and the cost of the paper, the folder, and any copywriting and design services. Fees for services can be minimized by doing it yourself (provided you can do it to professional standards) or hiring a reasonably priced freelance.

At the outset, a press kit is nice but not necessary. Until you have a sheaf of articles and reviews, the folder might appear a bit thin. Consider this tool when the material at hand justifies the effort and expense, including postage. Another increasingly popular tool to consider is the electronic, Web-based press kit. Journalists have easy access to the Web, which enables authors to update their press kits as needed and saves all parties from shuffling paper.

Advertising

The issue of whether to advertise a book generates controversy. Predictably, authors want advertising and publishers question its value. The question is legitimate. As an insightful businessman once said, "Half the money we spend on advertising is wasted. The trouble is, we don't know which half."

While advertising won't hurt a book's sales, it can, from the publisher's perspective, hurt its profitability. Furthermore, most publishers' primitive systems for tracking and analyzing sales tell them little about advertising's effectiveness. A print ad in the *New York Times*, *Wall Street Journal*, *Fortune*, or *Business Week* generates awareness. But does it generate more sales for a given title than ads in narrowly targeted publications? Does advertising generate more sales than a guest spot on NPR? No one really knows.

Co-op advertising may be more useful and is certainly more measurable. In co-op programs, the publisher and the bookstore share the cost of ads to pull customers into the store for specific books, which are usually discounted. Co-op advertising is closer to the customer and gets the bookseller involved in moving the title.

Should an author pay for advertising? It's among the most expensive tactics in the mix, and the returns are uncertain. Unless the publication is highly targeted and the ad space reasonably priced, a description that fits some newsletters and small magazines, it's better to put money into publicity efforts. Most people regard publicity, for which the publication receives no payment, as more credible than advertising, for which the publication is paid.

Postcards, Flyers, and Other Direct Mail

To impress customers and prospects, word of the book must get around. Mailing postcards or flyers before publication, even if you also intend to send complimentary books later, can create some early buzz.

Color postcards to announce the book can be printed for a little over a nickel apiece, plus $200 to $300 for a design based on the cover. Promotional book marks cost about the same. One-page color promotional flyers or one-sheets cost a bit over ten cents each, plus similar design fees, but they require more postage than postcards and (usually) an envelope. Black and white flyers cost considerably less, but also make less of an impression.

Aside from printing and design expenses, postage and handling are the only other costs involved in direct mail—if you have good customer and prospect mailing lists. If you don't, list development expenses add up. Although purchased mailing lists can be cheaper than developing your own lists, they will be less effective unless they focus directly on your target audience. Purchased lists (as opposed to those you develop yourself) can be quite inaccurate, with up to twenty percent or more "nixies"—out of date addresses, bankrupt companies, and the like. Membership lists of professional or industry associations may be more expensive than those compiled by list developers but, if they target the right audience, worth it.

In other words, mail aggressively to customer and prospect lists you have developed but carefully consider the value of direct mail to other lists.

Speaking Engagements

Speaking and writing books go hand in hand. They strongly reinforce one another. Public speaking also provides something many authors crave but rarely achieve—face-to-face contact with readers. What's more, undertaken professionally, speaking itself generates income. Companies and associations always need speakers for meetings and events. To command high fees however, you'll need first-rate speaking skills and a systematic marketing program. Otherwise you're competing with people who are working harder at it.

A different kind of speaking opportunity may be available through adult learning programs in your city, such as the Learning Annex in New York and Los Angeles and the Boston Center for Adult Education. In addition to the chance to speak before small but receptive audiences, there's always the free advertising of having the name of your book in the thousands of catalogs they distribute.

To market yourself as a speaker, you need collateral materials—background on yourself and the kinds of talks you give, a photograph, and a short videotaped speech. You also need a program of regular contact with conference producers, event planners, and industry and professional associations. If you produce enough income and have an easily marketable persona and presentation, consider listing with a speakers' bureau. For a percentage of your fees (usually twenty-five percent), the bureau will secure bookings and handle some of the administrative and logistical details. How aggressively they will market you depends on your past and potential speaking fees.

Hate travel? Then you may put your book at a disadvantage. Speaking represents a wide plank in the platform of most best-selling business book authors. It's an essential tactic for anyone who wants to sell lots of books, or the services of their company, or both.

Don't like public speaking? You need not be a silver-tongued devil. Most reasonably articulate business people can become comfortable enough with speaking to sell books. Join Toastmasters, get professional coaching—if necessary, hire a speechwriter. Many people, especially the biggest fans, want to see the person behind the book. That interchange sells books and builds an author's brand loyalty.

Start by reading a couple of good books on public speaking. Among the best are *Speak and Grow Rich* by Dottie and Lilly Walters, *Money Talks: How to Make a Million as a Speaker* by Alan Weiss, and *Getting Started in Speaking, Training or Seminar Consulting* by Robert W. Bly. Then troll *Gale's Directory of Associations* for organizations that a) cover your target audience and b) hold conferences. Mail your materials to the director, whose name should be listed. Better yet, call for the name of the person who books the speakers for their conferences and direct your materials to her.

When you land a speaking engagement:

- Instead of trying to explain the whole book, pick the chapter that would be most useful to the audience and build your talk around it. Use examples from their business or profession whenever possible.

- Don't hard-sell the book or your business. One way or another, people pay to attend events and they expect value, not a sales pitch (though a bit of soft selling is usually acceptable).

- Three weeks before the engagement, have enough copies of the book sent to a specific, reliable person who will deliver them to the right room. Ask the conference coordinator how many books to ship. Usually only a small percentage of the audience buys a copy.

- Five days before the engagement, ascertain that the books arrived in good condition and are where they are supposed to be.

Compensation ranges from nothing to expenses to honoraria of $50 to $500 to fees up to several thousand dollars, plus your share of any on-the-spot sales of the book. The real payoff of speaking comes over time as your reputation grows and sales of the book— and whatever else you are selling—increase. New authors should grab any opportunity to speak before the right group.

Book Parties and Book Tours

Money spent on a book party would probably be better spent elsewhere. If you have the space and can host the event, it won't hurt sales. But unless you are already a high-profile author who can get media coverage of the party, it's a low-return activity and would be even if the publisher were paying for it (which they won't). Publishers admit that they host book parties mainly to massage best-selling authors' egos.

A book tour takes the author to a number of cities (from three or four to twenty, thirty, or more) to meet with representatives of local print and broadcast media and to appear in bookstores. Most book tours are arranged by the publisher's staff publicist or a public relations firm. If your publisher is going to organize and fund a book tour, terrific. You need only show up as scheduled and bang the drum for your book.

Some authors mount their own tours. Is the payoff worth it? Setting up productive visits in multiple cities takes time, effort, and travel money. The value of the tour depends on your book, audience, and finances, and on your organizational and public relations skills. Without the publisher's support, it's best to "tour" your own city and cities within driving distance. Gauge how productive these mini-tours are, bearing in mind that success may come most easily in your own area, where you are a local author and know the territory.

Many bookstores host signings, readings, and seminars that showcase a book and its author. Whether you or your publisher funds a bookstore appearance, try to structure an "event" rather than a signing. In an event, you teach people something, entertain them, or provide a discussion forum. Teaming up with another author who has a related but different book can provide critical mass, if it's lacking, as can a "business book afternoon" arranged by the bookstore's community relations director. Although bookstore appearances may produce meager on-the-spot sales, having your name and book featured in the store's flyer provides ample advertising to a book-buying audience.

Authors with outgoing personalities "work" bookstores by schmoozing with the manager and staff, citing the book's benefits, signing copies of the book (which then can't be returned to the publisher), and even improving the display of their book. Be aware, however, that placement on the "new arrivals" table and other preferential spots is sold by the major chains, usually to major publishers.

Web-based Activities

Whether you are an author, expert-author, or collaborator, supporting your book and your business with a Web site doesn't just make sense: It has become a must. Among the many books that have been written on Web-based marketing, the one currently most focused on publicizing books is *Buzz Your Book* by M.J. Rose and Douglas Clegg. It's part of their *Buzz Your...* series of e-books (*Buzz Your Website*, *Buzz Your Zine*, and so on) and is downloadable for a reasonable price at www.buzzyour.com. Author-speaker-consultant Marcia Yudkin's *Internet Marketing for Less than $500/Year* is a superb all-round primer on Web-based marketing.

Fittingly enough, several Web sites provide solid, free information on Web-based promotion. Yudkin's site at www.yudkin.com has lots of good ideas and is itself a sterling example of effective Web-based marketing, as is consultant Alan Weiss' site at www.summit consulting.com. Dan Poynter's site, www.parapublishing.com, is a must-visit for anyone considering self-publishing. It also features ideas on promotion that any author can use. More specialized articles, including one on Amazon sales rankings and another on keywords that people search on (words that may help search engines access your site) can be found at www.fonerbooks.com, created and maintained by author and consultant Morris Rosenthal. A good search engine, such as www.google.com, can also help you locate sites relevant to your book, market, and the tactic you want to use.

If your business already maintains a Web site, you are that much ahead of the game. Just be sure to integrate the book and all book-related activities into the site. These would include news of any appearances you will be making, free and perhaps reasonably priced information related to the subject of your book, recent reviews of the book, and either an online ordering mechanism or a link to an online bookstore that carries your book.

A regular e-mail newsletter can help you stay in touch with members of your virtual community. Of course, like other forms of business communication, e-mail newsletters are reaching the saturation point, so keep it short. Marcia Yudkin's Marketing Minute, which is e-mailed every Wednesday, is a good example.

The real challenge in Web marketing and publicity is drawing people to your site. Be certain to have your URL (Uniform Resource Locator, also known as your Web-site address) on the back cover of your book, as well as on postcards, press releases, letterhead, business cards, brochures, and presentation handouts. When you write an article for a publication, secure *upfront* agreement that the brief biographical note at the end of the piece will include your URL and e-mail address. Speaking of e-mail, add a "signature" at the end of every e-mail you send. This should contain your contact information, including your Web-site address. Links to other Web sites that are related but not directly competitive with yours can bring in visitors. Either contact the site's Web master and discuss the possibility or proactively link them to your site and ask them if they will reciprocate.

To generate repeat visits, refresh your site regularly with new material, features, and links, and maintain a good amount of archived information. And make sure you report on your Web site any positive occurrence related to your book—reviews, speaking engagements, media coverage, and second, third, and subsequent printings and editions.

Product Extensions and Other Tactics

Successful business books can find second and third lives as audiobooks and in other forms. Audiobooks come in abridged and unabridged forms read by the author or by an actor or voice model. The publisher may sell the audio rights to an audiobook company, unless they have their own audiobook division, or you may sell the rights, if you retained them or they reverted to you. (Again, your book contract should state that any subsidiary rights assigned to the publisher revert to you after some period in which the publisher does not sell or exercise them, or when the book goes out of print.) Another option, if you own the rights, is to hire studio time, produce the recording yourself, and have tapes or CDs duplicated to sell or use as gifts or premiums.

Everything in the previous paragraph also applies to e-books, although technical issues could make producing and marketing one yourself a time-consuming task. Although as of this writing e-books have failed to win many readers, that could change.

Print and electronic newsletters represent a natural extension of a book. Fax-on-demand and downloadable Web-based reports and templates are other logical extensions to consider, as are workshops and seminars based on the book.

In general, think of yourself as an information provider and "repurpose" the information in your book in as many promotional and profitable ways as you can.

Working with the Staff Publicist

Every book, article, and speaker on the topic of book promotion will say, "Be sure to coordinate your publicity plan for your book with your publisher!" This statement implies that the publisher has a promotion plan for the book. In truth, that "plan" is usually to a) ask the author where to send review copies of the book and then to send them, b) send copies to the house's list of reviewers, and c) write a press release and send it to the house's and author's media lists. That's it.

Some authors withhold their plan from the publisher because they think that the publisher will not feel obligated to promote the book if the author is already doing so. The reality is that nothing is going to make the publisher feel obligated to promote a book vigorously unless the author already has a solid track record. Go ahead and share your promotion plan with your editor. At the very least it will demonstrate that you'll be promoting the book. It's also a matter of courtesy. However, the "coordinating" to be done will be minimal, unless the publisher is actively promoting the book.

Even then, the reason for exhorting authors to coordinate their plans with the publisher remains elusive. What's the issue? Without coordination, the author might wind up being double-booked on National Public Radio? Or have two articles pitched to *Inc.* magazine? We should have such lack of coordination.

The cardinal rule is this: Never rely on the publisher to do much beyond sending out review copies and a press release. By all means, ask to talk with staff publicists and meet them if possible. Give them a synopsis of the book, a positioning statement, and story angles for various publications and media. Keep in touch. Write thank you notes and complimentary letters when they land a review or an interview. (Sending flowers has been known to help.) But consider whatever they do to be gravy.

Should You Hire a PR Firm or Book Publicist?
If you lack the money to hire a PR firm or book publicist, the question is moot, so let's first consider the expense. Depending on the level and type of services you want, hiring a small firm will cost $3,000 to $4,500 for three months, but add another two months to cover publications with long lead times. That brings

the total to $5,000 to $7,000. This implies a monthly rate of $1,000 to $1,500, but PR firms need at least three months to get results.

Although you can specify services you want, these rates include writing and sending a press release, sending advance mailings of galleys with a cover letter written by a copywriter at the firm, sending review copies, and making follow-up calls. Adding more services, such as placing articles in selected publications or broadening the scope to national publicity can bring the total figure to $15,000. Fees for ghostwritten articles would be another extra.

For a book tour, the publicist will book radio, television, and press interviews and appearances for a fee ranging from $1,500 to $3,000 per city. The higher end of that range applies to larger cities, which have more media outlets.

The fees of freelance book publicists also range widely, from a few hundred dollars for a half-day consult to project fees or monthly retainers, depending on the level of service you want and the record of the publicist.

If you have the money and you need the ideas, skills, or resources that a PR firm can provide, then consider hiring one. If your publisher frankly admits that they don't plan on doing any promotion, the rationale for hiring a publicist becomes even stronger. Talk with a few firms or freelance publicists who have *experience promoting business books*. Part of what you're buying is the firm's access to editors and producers. You are also buying their ability to plan and execute a mix of the tactics outlined in this chapter. This should include pitches tailored and targeted to specific publications and radio and television programs, rather than a one-size-fits-all approach.

Some book publicists admit that they really cannot do anything you cannot do. They may get their phone calls to media people returned more quickly, or have a bit of leverage with an editor or producer, but publicists with big-time clout are few. (They are also expensive: Fees for "big books" by proven authors and celebrity-CEOs range up to $50,000 and well beyond). However, any good, experienced book publicist will get the word out for you if you are too busy or lack the marketing skills.

As with any professional, you must trust the publicist and feel some rapport. You are giving up a measure of control over the promotion effort and must be comfortable doing that. Know too that publicists cannot work miracles. The more promotable and topical your book is, the better they will perform, but they cannot force editors and producers to run a piece on a book. Although a good publicist will generate great ideas and execute them well, they can't promise their clients a placement in the *Wall Street Journal*.

Ask your editor to recommend two or three publicists suited to your book. You don't have to hire one suggested by the editor, but the publicist and the editor's team should be able to work together, if the occasion arises. Keep in touch with your publicist for regular updates on which media are being approached and with what results. If the publisher hires a publicity firm or freelance promoter, that's an excellent sign. It rarely happens for a first-time or midlist business book author. If it does, establish a relationship with the publicist and be as involved and responsive as possible.

The Budget
Developing a "time budget" as well as a monetary budget enables you to consider the total resource commitment to promoting the book. It also highlights the trade-offs between time and money. If you are a consultant, for instance, does it really cost more to job out a mailing if doing it yourself will reduce your billable hours? Should certain publicity tasks be delegated to an independent contractor? The budgeting process won't answer every question. But it will provide a framework for answering them, as well as guidelines for action after the book is launched.

Ready, Aim, Fire, Fire, Fire

The following steps lead to effective decisions regarding promotional resources:

- Estimate the total hours and dollars available for the effort
- Identify the specific promotional activities to undertake
- Estimate the hours and dollars required for each activity
- Weigh the potential trade-offs among the activities
- Develop final budgets for each activity and the overall effort

Estimate Total Hours and Dollars

Time and money are interchangeable in some marketing activities. An author can either research publications, write query letters, assemble mailings, telephone editors, and write articles—or pay someone to do these things. The author himself must be available for other activities, such as interviews, speaking engagements, and bookstore appearances.

Each author must allocate time and money to promotion according to her goals, means, and situation. For instance, if a consultant consistently bills out at $1,500 a day, then a week on the road touting the book "costs" $7,500, in addition to travel expenses. That forgone $7,500 doesn't represent a true, tax-deductible cash outlay and therefore shouldn't appear in the budget. However, it should be considered.

A realistic allocation of time to promote a book aggressively in the four months before and the six months after publication would range from four hundred to six hundred hours. This translates to forty to sixty hours a month, with pre-publication efforts devoted mainly to mailing postcards, letters, and blads to generate awareness of the book and to sending query letters to magazines and newsletters. The expert-author promoting a business should also launch pre-publication mailings to customers and prospects. The time after publication will be devoted more to interviews and appearances, queries to newspapers, and pitches to producers. Throughout the promotional effort, some weeks are likely to be heavier than others.

The money allocated to promotion can range from shoestring budgets of $1,000 for mailings, phone calls, and minimal travel to $15,000 monthly retainers for publicists, plus fees for ghostwriters of articles and speeches. A reasonable range for an aggressive but largely internal effort would be $5,000 to $10,000. However, unless they are well-controlled, travel expenses, Web-site design, and "free" books (purchased at the author's discount) could easily triple those numbers.

It is essential, then, to view the expenditures of time and money as an investment and to allocate these resources to high-return activities. Be mindful of your reasons for writing the book. A book that is meant to boost the business of a specialized consulting firm may do its job just by getting into the hands of the top five hundred people positioned to hire the firm. In that case, expensive efforts to reach other readers may be overkill. On the other hand, a book meant to establish a writer as a business book author may need to reach a wider audience and draw some favorable reviews. Of course, every author would like to have a best seller, but realistically scaling and tailoring your PR efforts to your goals in writing the book will yield the best bang for the buck.

Identify Specific Activities

With rough budget numbers in hand, it's time to identify the most promising promotional activities, the ones that will be most effective given your book, target audience, skills, personality, schedule, funds, and goals.

Essentials include press releases to most potentially interested parties, query letters to editors, pitch letters to producers, mailings to clients and prospects (some with free copies of the book), follow-up phone calls to promising editors and producers, and at least local speaking engagements.

Plan to work all local venues—print, broadcast, cable, bookstores, companies, and associations—thoroughly. Beyond the local area, plan to pursue appearances in cities within 250 miles or so. Effective promotion of this type can generate regional sales and perhaps a regional hit. From that base, or simultaneously, you can move to other regions.

Estimate Hours and Dollars for Each Activity

Next, determine the amount of time and money it will take to implement each tactic you plan to undertake. These amounts will depend on what the tactics are and the degree to which you already do them. If you regularly contact a list of customers and prospects, for example, direct mail will require less incremental time and money than if you don't.

The scale of the activity affects costs even more. Fortunately, most promotional activities can be started small and scaled up as desired. You can approach a few bookstores or send a mailing to five hundred people. You can start with a small five-page Web site and grow it from there, or speak in front of regional chapters of an association before approaching the national organization. As each tactic succeeds or fails, scale it up or back accordingly.

Accurately estimating the expense of these tactics calls for research and analysis. It means talking to printers, calculating direct-mail expenses, investigating periodicals and broadcast venues, and forecasting travel expenses. A budget developed without that foundation isn't a budget—it's a guess.

Weigh Trade-offs among Activities

Now consider the relative costs and benefits of the selected activities. Where can you make trade-offs between more and less time-consuming and more or less costly activities? Would postcards be cheaper than letters but work as well for some audiences? Should you approach lower-circulation business periodicals before taking a run at the larger ones? Is advertising in a newsletter that reaches your audience something to reconsider?

Using a marketing mix enables you to trade off among activities. Thinking through the potential trade-offs beforehand makes future decisions easier because you have already considered the relative costs and benefits.

Develop Final Budgets

Finally, construct a budget that gives you flexibility as well as control over your time and money. The budgeted amounts may be expressed as either point estimates or ranges. *Some* elements of a sample starter budget for an author performing all tasks himself (except putting material on the Web site) are shown in the table on the following page.

Although the program can be scaled up or back as results play out, don't give up too quickly on a promotional activity. Some of them, such as efforts to land speaking engagements, bear fruit only after multiple attempts. Try different approaches with successive contacts—highlighting different aspects of the book, for instance—and eventually you will find hot buttons.

Scheduling, Timing, and Execution

You cannot do everything at once, nor should you. Some activities pave the way for others or are time-sensitive. The following suggested schedule will help you launch activities when they will do the most good:

Six to Nine Months before Publication

Planning should begin at least six months before publication. This

Starter Budget		
Task	*Expense*	*Time*
Mail copies of book to all 25 clients & top-75 prospects	$1,400	7 hours
Mail 500 specialty postcards to other clients & prospects	255	6 hours
Prepare & send query letters to 20 periodicals & 50 newspapers	50	25 hours
Follow up query letters with phone calls	45	12 hours
At our existing Web site, set up section on the book & an ordering mechanism	800	9 hours

means identifying and prioritizing magazines, newsletters, broadcast and cable media, industry and professional associations, and other venues, along with the names and contact information of the people to approach. It also means going through the budgeting process outlined above.

Conferences operate on the longest lead times. Speakers for annual conferences for major associations are booked many months in advance.

Talk to two or three business book publicists and Web-site designers and hosts during this time to gauge their services and expenses.

Three to Six Months before Publication

Magazines operate on the next-longest lead time. Monthly magazines are put to bed about three months in advance, while newsletters operate on slightly shorter schedules. Special issues of periodicals—such as the small business issue or the technology issue—are planned far in advance so that the periodical's advertising sales people can secure early commitments from advertisers to buy space. (Request magazines' editorial calendars and author's guidelines well in advance.)

If you plan to hire freelance writers to produce articles, or any other independent contractors, start lining them up. Hire a Website designer and host and start developing the site.

Secure dust-jacket blurbs and send blads or bound galleys to book-review editors at business magazines and to bookstores with strong business book sections. Begin to establish relationships with key bookstores, including online bookstores.

Plan, write copy, and prepare any necessary artwork for advertisements, if applicable, and for postcards, flyers, and other material to be distributed.

Draft query letters for editors and producers.

Three to Six Weeks before Publication
Launch the Web site and begin efforts to draw users to it. Mail query letters to newspapers and pitch letters to producers. Mail postcards, flyers, and letters to clients, prospects, colleagues, and friends. Line up appearances at bookstores.

Upon and After Publication
Continue all print and broadcast activities, expanding to wider audiences and other regions as desired. Continue to pursue speaking engagements. Work with bookstores to arrange events and connect with the staff.

As articles appear, obtain reprints and send them to clients, prospects, and associations.

Build the perception of momentum and success. Remain relentlessly positive. Ignore any bad reviews of the book. If someone tells you about a bad review, shrug it off as part of the game or briefly point out why it's wrong, then mention a positive review or development.

Don't throw money around, but don't let up either. Capitalize on anything positive that occurs—a review, article, speaking engagement, or increase in sales—by getting word out to clients, prospects, and the target audiences for the book.

Using a Book to Promote a Business

By now you know that a book should be considered one element in a company's marketing mix. A book makes a statement: "We have been to the top of the mountain (of leadership, innovation, quality control, customer service, or whatever) and here's what we learned!" That's news, and because it's news, the book generates interviews, articles, and speaking engagements. The book drives the company's overall marketing mix; the marketing mix also sells the book. However, on its own a book cannot be expected to generate sales for the business—only awareness of and interest in the business. It takes hard work to convert awareness and interest into sales.

Pushing the Business, Gently

Effective expert-authors market the business when they market the book. This calls for a sense of balance. The public expects the author to be a business person, but at the same time, they don't want to be pounded by sales messages. So the expert-author must sell subtly. In media interviews and Q&A sessions, answer questions in terms of your business. Useful phrases include: "our customers are seeing…," "our suppliers tell us…," "in our foreign markets—that is, in South America—conditions are improving…," "everything in our experience at Acme showed that…." It's natural for business people to talk about their companies, customers, suppliers, markets, and initiatives.

In articles, weave your company lightly into the fabric of the piece. An article with a customer case-study shows your business in action. This brings the subject to life and increases reader recall. It also boosts your credibility while giving the reader practical information, including information about your company's capabilities.

Build up other people in your company. Mentioning that your vice president, Joyce Johnson, has been a genius at integrating customers' systems or that you have the best quality assurance manager in your industry showcases the company's talent and keeps the business front and center.

Casually mentioning the company will smooth the move toward any overt selling you do get to do. Suppose an interviewer invites a plug, for example by asking, "What should CEOs do if all else fails?" The answer—"Call us or visit our Web site"—will be more natural and have greater impact if you have already referred to the business a couple of times.

Sparking Sales with the Book

The following steps will boost the value of a book as a sales tool:

- Have your company contact information and a general description of your business on one page at the back of the book itself. Some authors do a lot of selling on this page, while others take a low-key approach. Look over several books and decide what works for you.

- Get the book into the right hands. Send a copy to decision makers at companies you want to cultivate. In a personally signed cover letter, point out specific parts of the book that will be of interest.

- Follow up after a week or two to introduce yourself. Avoid putting the prospect on the spot about whether he read the book. Instead, explain that you would like to explore the possibility of doing business with him and why.

- Spin material from the book into other forms, such as executive briefings, a quarterly newsletter, or Web-based content. Send out article reprints, announcements of upcoming media appearances, and press releases about the book's success. By way of follow-up, phone or e-mail the best prospects among these recipients.
- Update your Web site once a week with material from the sources just noted. Also, use every available vehicle to draw users to the site.
- Request responses and comments about the book from readers, customers, and prospects. Comb these comments for ideas and leads. But weed out unqualified prospects who seek a free education or otherwise want to kill time. Politely refer them to your book, Web site, or other sources.

Treat prospects surfaced by your book as you would those found through other lead generating activities. Ask questions about their business, problems, and needs and ascertain their ability and willingness to pay for solutions you can provide. The difference between actual prospects and the merely interested emerges quickly. Move actual prospects into your sales process. If they need a follow-up phone call, an on-site visit, a work sample, or product literature, make sure they receive it and that follow-up continues. And just in case all of this works, have resources ready to deal with any increase in business.

Ultimately, the book forms a major plank in a platform on which you stand above competitors who do not have the compelling messages you have communicated. The rest of that platform comprises an ongoing campaign of ever greater reach into your target markets. As the saying goes, "It's a process, not an event." Granted, the book is an event, and a happy one, but there is a reason that successful expert-authors often publish more than one book. They found it was worthwhile and they believe it will be worthwhile the second and third time. They see publishing a book as one more marketing activity and believe that, as in all marketing, repetition increases returns.

Ever Onward

The business book genre represents a vital segment of publishing. The category encompasses a huge range of material: how-to, self-help, journalism, scholarship, and even humor and inspiration. Best sellers and backlist favorites regularly spring from the business genre.

For business people and professional writers, these books offer a realistic path to publication, along with the risks and rewards of writing and publishing any book. Despite the consolidation and the ups and downs that have occurred in book publishing, even the major business book houses and imprints remain open to new ideas and new authors. Moreover, the alternatives to publishing with a major house have never been more numerous or viable. A good number of small publishers specialize in business books, moving in where larger publishers fear to tread or tread too slowly. Self-publishing and publishers of professional/technical books open doors for the author with specialized material aimed at smaller, easily targeted audiences. For the determined business book author, there is always a way into print, and there will be for the foreseeable future.

One final tip: Ignore people who enjoy running down the book business. Book publishing has been a dying industry since the day Johann Gutenberg cranked up his press to run off something other than the Bible. Yet books don't go away, and they won't go away. Their form is perfect for their function. Their value often outweighs their price. And their ability to communicate ideas from one mind to another remains irresistible to both parties in the author-reader transaction.

About
Tom Gorman and
Content Publishing

Tom Gorman has written, co-authored, and collaborated on a dozen business books and numerous articles, white papers, and executive briefings. He is the author of the career management guide *Multipreneuring* (Simon & Shuster) and *The Complete Idiot's Guide to Economics, The Complete Idiot's Guide to MBA Basics*, and *The Complete Idiot's Almanac of Business Letters and Memos* (Alpha Books).

He is the coauthor, with Paul C. Miller, Ph.D., of *Big League Business Thinking* (Prentice Hall) and, with Tom Richardson and Augusto Vidaurreta, of *Business Is a Contact Sport* (Alpha Books). As an uncredited collaborator, he has developed and written books published by Prentice Hall, Amacom Books, and Career Press. He also researched and wrote a corporate history for a major U.S. financial institution.

Content Publishing works with consultants, executives, entrepreneurs, and experts who want to have a business book published. These books are sold in bookstores and are used by their authors to document their organizations' practices, communicate with stakeholders, and promote sales.

Services include ghostwriting and collaborating with authors on *commercially viable* business book proposals and manuscripts for consulting firms, companies, financial institutions, associations, literary agents, and editors. Tom Gorman regularly speaks to gatherings of business people and writers on developing, writing, and publishing business books. To learn more, visit our Web site, call the number below, or send a query letter (rather than a proposal or manuscript) to:

Content Publishing
1075 Washington Street
Newton, MA 02465
617-558-5800
www.contentbizbooks.com

Appendix I

Sample Business Book Proposal

 The following proposal for *Business Is a Contact Sport* by Tom Richardson and Augusto Vidaurreta with Tom Gorman was sold to Alpha Books in 2000. The proposal omits the introduction and sample chapter, which have since been published in the book itself. There have also been a few minor edits to disguise or omit the names of actual companies that were cited as examples in the proposal but not in the book. Otherwise, the proposal is presented here as it was presented to editors at business book publishers.

This sample proposal is not presented as an industry standard in terms of approach or format. It is simply an approach and format that has worked for me and my clients.

Business Is a Contact Sport was published in hardcover by Alpha Books, a company of Pearson Education, in autumn 2001.

Business Is a Contact Sport

Using the 12 Principles of Relationship Asset Management to Build Buy-in, Blast away Barriers, and Boost Your Business

by
Tom Richardson
and
Augusto Vidaurreta

with Tom Gorman

Table of Contents of the Proposal

Executive Summary

About the Book
- Going Beyond Customers and Employees
- Seeing Relationships as Assets
- Turning Bystanders into Stakeholders

Market Assessment
- Target Market
- Competitive Books
- Where *Business Is a Contact Sport* Fits

About the Authors

About the Writing Collaborator

Specifications of the Book

Table of Contents of the Book

Chapter Summaries

Introduction and Sample Chapter [not included here]

Executive Summary

Vince Lombardi's famous saying, "Winning isn't everything. It's the only thing," summed up an approach to football—a contact sport if ever there were one—and to business that appeals to many people. We can't argue with Lombardi's record in football, but in business we've found that a different approach leads to greater success. Our approach focuses on winning, but also on helping everyone else to win along with you.

Business is a contact sport because human contact, connection, and cooperation is the essence of business. Even in our transaction-driven, increasingly virtual world, solid, long-lasting relationships are still fundamental to success. Yet in most companies, relationships—with customers and employees, and even more so with suppliers, distributors, licensees, licensors, shareholders, lenders, strategic partners, board members, universities, charities, the media, and the community—are the most underutilized assets.

Tom Richardson and Augusto Vidaurreta believe that managers and entrepreneurs must recognize *all* of their company's relationships as strategic assets, and manage them as such. The authors believe that relationships are so important that in the future the valuation of a company will include an analysis of the value of its relationships with all stakeholders. Therefore these successful consultants and entrepreneurs have developed a system for managing every business relationship as an asset, which they present in *Business Is a Contact Sport: Using the 12 Principles of Relationship Asset Management to Build Buy-in, Blast away Barriers, and Boost Your Business*.

In *Business Is a Contact Sport* readers will:

- learn how to initiate and build solid, supportive relationships with everyone they deal with in business
- develop strategies for putting relationships to work for their company and for themselves, so they can reach their goals

- discover a win-centric system they can apply throughout their organizations that will maximize the mutual value of every relationship.

In contrast to other books, this one views *every* relationship as valuable and manageable. Many books are devoted to customer service; many others to employee relations. Still others focus on the board of directors or the media. *Business Is a Contact Sport* treats all relationships as interdependent, in the context of a relationship web.

This reflects reality. In our connected, media-driven world, any irate customer, disgruntled employee, activist shareholder, zealous regulator, or wronged member of the community can grab an open mike and sound off. On the other hand, good news—particularly very good news—also travels fast, to a company's lasting benefit.

In *Business Is a Contact Sport*, Tom Richardson and Augusto Vidaurreta reveal ways of managing all business relationships for maximum *mutual* benefit. The result? A book that shows readers how to develop valuable, long-term relationships with all of their company's stakeholders—which means greater opportunity, revenue, income, and protection from downside risk.

About the Book

Whether the world is getting smaller, faster, more connected, or more fragmented—or all of the above—most observers agree that traditional business relationships are changing rapidly, and not necessarily for the better. The evidence includes:

- Waning employee loyalty driven by downsizing, layoffs, reduced benefits and a newly knowledgeable, independent, satisfaction-seeking workforce
- Customers in search of the best deal on every transaction,

with quality, speed, service, compatibility, or price defining "best" depending on their need at that moment on that day

- Disintermediation between buyers and sellers, due to the pace of change, crumbling boundaries, and new ways of doing business, particularly on the Internet
- New competitors who, thanks to new technologies, widespread deregulation, and lower trade-barriers, come out of nowhere.

Conglomeratization, globalization, materialism, short-term thinking, and technology have all been charged with crimes against relationships. Whatever the cause, this much is clear: the characteristics of business relationships are changing rapidly.

However, human nature has not changed. The human need for contact, interaction, and affiliation, for respect, recognition, and reward, for teamwork, sharing, and mutual benefit, have not diminished. They are constants, and because they are constants, relationships between people remain at the heart of the human endeavor known as business.

What does this mean to managers and entrepreneurs? Opportunity! Because companies that develop and maintain strong relationships will, on a variety of dimensions, outperform those that don't.

Going Beyond Customers and Employees

Most managers, when they seriously consider business relationships, consider only those with customers and employees. While this limited thinking needs to change, it is understandable.

The positive effects of strong customer relationships have been well documented. In a *Harvard Business Review* article called "Preventing the Premature Death of Relationship Marketing" (Jan.-Feb. 1998), Fournier, Dobscha, and Mick cited companies who found that their most loyal customers, the top 20 percent, provided all of their profits and actually covered the losses incurred in dealing with less loyal customers. Separately, Xerox has found that customers who rate themselves "very satisfied" were six times more likely to buy Xerox equipment again than "satisfied" customers.

The benefits of solid employee relationships have also been extolled. In a ten-year study, Bill Catlette and Richard Hadden, authors of *Contented Cows Give Better Milk: The Plain Truth about Employee Relations and Your Bottom Line*, discovered that companies with high levels of employee satisfaction outgrew those with lower levels by almost four to one. Net income growth of the high-satisfaction companies was 202 percent versus 139 percent for the low-satisfaction ones. Most strikingly, the happier employees produced average sales-per-employee of $550,000 versus $165,000 for the less contented group.

We strongly believe in strong customer and employee relationships. On the customer-relations front at our own company, Systems Consulting Group (SCG), an information-technology consulting firm, we landed and retained national and international accounts, *with no sales force* usually on the basis of referrals. On the employee-relations front, in an industry plagued by annual turnover of 20 to 30 percent, ours averaged six to seven percent annually over the eight years we managed the firm.

Although managers see the importance of good customer and employee relations, to sustain success today, they must broaden their view of "important relationships" to include all relationships. They must bring the same focus they try to bring to customer and employee relationships to relationships with everyone the company touches. In addition, managers need a system for doing this, for managing relationships as the valuable assets they truly are.

The need for management to broaden its view stems from the

nature of relationships in the changing business landscape. Every stakeholder is valuable, and too great a focus on any single constituency without considering the impact on other stakeholders will warp behavior and create imbalances. For instance, management at many publicly held companies constantly caters to Wall Street. Driven by the stock market, they myopically pursue short-term earnings growth and in the process sacrifice employee bonuses, R&D, and other elements important to the company's long-term health. This in effect places the need of one group, shareholders, above the needs of all other stakeholders. Employee compensation, customer satisfaction, even investment for the company's future, become secondary. Management may mouth platitudes—"People are our most important asset" and "The customer is king"—however, employees and customers are not fooled. They eventually leave and when they do, the task of hitting quarterly earnings targets becomes impossible.

The need for a system for managing relationships became clear to us in establishing and growing SCG through most of the past decade. As former consultants with Arthur Andersen, we found a systems approach to most tasks comfortable and effective. As entrepreneurs and managers we found such an approach to be the only way to address all the needs of everyone we had to deal with in what became, by most measures and certainly for us, a sizable enterprise.

By character and temperament, we've never been able to say, "Forget this guy. He's of no value to us." We were always looking for the long-term value in a relationship. Maybe we were well-reared by our parents. Or maybe we simply realized that the guy looking for a job or soliciting a donation for a charity today might be a customer or a reporter from the *Miami Herald* tomorrow. In other words, that person, or more accurately the relationship with that person, was an asset or potential asset, to our company. Yet we found managing the array of relationships we formed as our company grew exponentially to be impossible without a system. We developed a system, and we call that system Relationship Asset Management or RAM™.

Seeing Relationships as Assets

To manage relationships as assets, you must see them as assets. Therefore, RAM calls for a shift in attitude and then a shift in behavior. It calls for strategy, then implementation.

In today's bottom-line driven, technologically focused business world, relationships are usually not seen as assets and thus are often squandered, undeveloped, and unmanaged. They resemble untilled acres of land, rusted machinery, abandoned buildings, and money under the mattress. For example, in far too many companies long-standing customers can leave and start purchasing elsewhere and nobody will call to ask them why. Similarly, employees' ideas go unsolicited, and when offered, go unrewarded. Investors and lenders are thought of as ATMs, until sales skid and cash flow tightens and they must be placated and cajoled. Adversarial purchasing managers mercilessly play suppliers off one another, then wonder why their company suffers during supply shortages or tight delivery times. The problems and wishes of local neighbors are ignored, until they reach crisis proportions. Universities, repositories of brainpower as well as manpower, are thought of as remote ivory towers.

To the extent that these or similar attitudes exist in a company, they must shift, and they can shift with the "asset management" approach that RAM embodies. This begins with understanding the role each relationship plays in helping the company enhance key success factors, minimize risks, and reach goals. That, after all, is the true value of a relationship as a business asset.

Then another shift must occur, toward a commitment to maximize the *mutual* benefits of the relationship. Thinking about, planning for, and consistently achieving wins for all parties represents the surest path to sustainable growth and high profits. This runs counter to the win-lose, zero-sum view of business relationships that many business people hold. Yet RAM creates faster growth and greater profits than competitive, zero-sum approaches.

Turning Bystanders into Stakeholders

Ultimately behavior, the way people are treated, must also change to reflect the value of relationship assets and the goal of maximizing mutual benefits. One of the first steps must be to appoint or recognize an "owner" of the relationship. Just as financial managers and facilities managers are responsible for specific assets, so too are relationship managers. We also recommend the appointment of a chief relationship officer to oversee relationship assets just as the chief financial officer and chief operating officer oversee financial and tangible assets.

Another useful step is to change both the frequency and character of communications. For instance, when a customer takes his business elsewhere, the relationship owner must call and learn why, and perhaps take measures to win that customer back now or to lay the groundwork to do so in the future. Suppliers and investors must receive more detailed information about the company's plans. Likewise, employees must be fully informed about the company's business and competitive situation, and asked for ideas for improvement. All of this transforms bystanders into stakeholders.

The broad steps in Relationship Asset Management are to:
1. Identify, evaluate, and prioritize all relationship assets
2. Recognize or assign an owner of the relationship
3. Define wins for the company and wins for the other party in each relationship

4. Move the relationship into the win-win zone, and keep it there.

This program, which we developed at SCG and use in our current enterprises, works. In fact we've seen it work so well that in late 1999 we established a venture-capital, mentor-capital, incubator firm called Entente, from the French word for an alliance. Entente employs the principles of Relationship Asset Management to turbocharge the usual investing and mentoring activities of such a firm.

Entente invests in startups and small companies, takes a position on their boards, and provides advice as needed. Added to that—as the turbocharger—are the principles of Relationship Asset Management, which generates synergy among member companies and among their stakeholders. RAM enables these companies to share resources, personnel, business practices, technology, even sales leads. They create joint proposals and win business they couldn't even bid on alone. Thus Entente member firms enjoy the best of both worlds. They are entrepreneurial and, through links created by RAM, have the power of a larger company.

RAM worked for us at SCG, creating wins for us and for all stakeholders. It is now doing the same for Entente members and their stakeholders. RAM will work in any organization of any size. It works because it serves the organizational need for revenue and income growth, for systematic approaches, and for capturing and maximizing value. RAM also works because it serves the individual need for contact, recognition, affiliation, teamwork, harmony, and rewards.

In *Business Is a Contact Sport* we will show readers how to replicate this system and realize its benefits in their own organizations.

Market Assessment

That relationships in general are under siege in this Age of the

Individual is hardly news in publishing circles. In the personal self-help category, "relationship books" represent a genre unto themselves. However few, if any, business books examine the relationships of an enterprise in their totality. *Business Is a Contact Sport* is, to our knowledge, the first book to do so. This does not, of course, mean that the book faces no competition, nor that it can appeal to everyone in the marketplace. We have, however, conceived and written a book that targets a huge audience and that has unique, built-in sales advantages over competitive books.

Target Market

Our primary target market is middle-to-senior level managers, entrepreneurs, and owners in companies of all sizes, and aspirants to those positions. Our secondary target market comprises human resources professionals, consultants, the nonprofit sector, and business people in general, this last group including professionals and employees at all levels as well as students and job seekers. Our target readers, especially managers, entrepreneurs, and business owners, are motivated by a desire to understand the "magic" by which some of us know "the right people," and develop relationships that, as we promise in the subtitle, build buy-in, blast away barriers, and boost their business. We're setting the bar high in terms of our promise to the reader because "the right people"—people who can help them reach their goals—are the true key to their success.

We also see a place for our book in business education, particularly at the graduate level. Special targets for *Business Is a Contact Sport* include the increasing number of MBA programs with courses in entrepreneurship. We also see a place for Relationship Asset Management in traditional and updated strategic planning courses. Business schools' traditional reluctance to add new methods to the curriculum has changed in recent years as evidenced by courses in leadership, managing technology, and balancing work and family.

Co-author Augusto Vidaurreta has taught as a guest lecturer at the University of Miami Graduate School of Management several times and still speaks at his alma mater. Both he and Tom Richardson have nurtured continuing relationships with Florida graduate schools of business. The authors intend to leverage these relationships to draw attention to their book and to their approach in business schools across the nation.

In fact, the authors have already begun this process. In early spring, they gave a lecture on Relationship Asset Management to the MBA Society at Florida International University. This was so well received that FIU is offering a course in RAM in its graduate business program this summer, with the authors as guest lecturers to supplement the professor teaching the course. (The dean of FIU has written that, "Relationship Asset Management accurately formalizes what successful companies have done intuitively.")

We expect *Business Is a Contact Sport* to appeal to women in that it focuses on the personal side of business and taps the concern most women have with professional, as well as personal, relationships. We are fully aware that 60 to 70 percent of trade books are purchased by women. Given the increasing number of women participating in sports at informal, amateur, and professional levels, we believe the sports metaphor—to be *lightly* woven through the material—will be an attractive selling point.

This book is aimed at everyone who wants to improve the efficiency and effectiveness of their business. It targets everyone who wants to improve profits, reduce employee turnover, increase customer retention, improve supplier performance, raise investor awareness, upgrade alliances with partners, and heighten their standing in the community and with the media. Whatever the business goal, *Business Is a Contact Sport* can help the reader achieve it, for the simple reason that business runs on relationships.

Competitive Books

Business Is a Contact Sport faces fragmented competition. Many current books present methods for initiating and maintaining a specific type of business relationship, most commonly those with employees and customers. Other individual books are devoted to relations with suppliers, shareholders, boards of directors, the community, and the media. No other book we could find in (or out of) print presents a program for managing the full spectrum of relationships, and for managing them as assets. (One book that may be viewed as more directly competitive, *Relationship Marketing*, covered below, focuses on customers and "discusses" other relationships.)

Improving customer relations has been the focus of many books. Among the more successful have been *The Loyalty Effect: The Hidden Force Behind Growth, Profits, and Lasting Value* by Frederick F. Reichheld (Harvard Business School Press, 1996). This book lays out the case for building customer loyalty even in these flighty times, as does *Customer Loyalty: How to Earn It, How to Keep It* by Jill Griffin (Jossey-Bass, 1997). Both *The One to One Future: Building Relationships One Customer at a Time* by Don Peppers and Martha Rogers (Bantam Doubleday Dell, 1997) and *Permission Marketing* by Seth Godin and Don Peppers (Simon & Schuster, 1999) scored well by taking readers beyond mass marketing to building relationships with customers as individuals. All of these books recommend the basic strategy of relationship marketing, forging partnerships with customers as individuals and selling and servicing them within the framework of that relationship.

The closest direct competitor to *Business Is a Contact Sport* is the successful *Relationship Marketing: New Strategies, Techniques and Technologies to Win the Customers You Want and Keep Them Forever* by Ian H. Gordon (John Wiley & Sons, 1998), which shows how top companies practice relationship marketing. According to Wiley, it also "discusses the hottest new spin on relationship marketing—relationship management, or the forging of relationships with investors, suppliers and employees, as well as customers." *Business Is a Contact Sport* goes much further, first, by taking a value-enhancing, "asset management" approach and, second, by extending it to every constituency of the company. The main focus of *Relationship Marketing* is customer relationships. Ours is all relationships.

Numerous books aim to help managers manage employees effectively. *The Human Equation: Building Profits by Putting People First* by Jeffrey Pfeffer (Harvard Business School Press, 1998) decries the rupture of the employer-employee social contract and puts forth a plan for fixing it. *Contented Cows Give Better Milk: The Plain Truth About Employee Relations and Your Bottom Line* by Bill Catlette and Richard Hadden (Williford Communications, 1998) does the same, as does *Keeping Good People: Strategies for Solving the #1 Problem Facing Business Today* by Roger E. Herman (Oak Hill Press, 1999). Crossing over into the (somewhat related) leadership-book category we have *The Passionate Organization: Igniting the Fire of Employee Commitment* by James R. Lucas (Amacom, 1999).

To its credit, *The Loyalty Link: How Loyal Employees Create Loyal Customers* by Dennis G. McCarthy (Wiley & Sons, 1997) does connect the management of employees with customer relations. However, it omits other business relationships. Our approach strengthens the links between and among all stakeholders, across what we call the Relationship Web.™

Relationships with investors have received little coverage in business books, which is odd given that they typically bear the blame for management's focus on short-term earnings and stock price. The books that do devote themselves to shareholder relations usually stress ways of "telling your story to investors." These include *New Dimensions in Investor Relations* by Bruce W. Marcus and Sherwood Lee Wallace (Wiley & Sons, 1997) and *Selling Your Story to Wall Street: The Art & Science of Investor Relations* by Michael A. Rosenbaum (Probus Publishing, 1994).

The investors' representatives, the board of directors, have been treated in various books from various perspectives. These tend to cover relations with boards either from the operating standpoint, such as *Boards at Work: How Corporate Boards Create Competitive Advantage* by Ram Charan (Jossey-Bass, 1998) and *Corporate Leadership: Boards, Directors, and Strategy* (McGraw-Hill, 1998), or from the corporate-governance standpoint, such as *The Board of Directors: 25 Keys to Corporate Governance* by Marianne Jennings (New York Times Pocket MBA Series, 1999).

Strategic partnerships and alliances have become commonplace in business, and business books reflect that fact. Successful books here include *Alliance Advantage: The Art of Creating Value through Partnering* by Yves L. Doz and Gary Hamel (Harvard Business School Press, 1998) and *Building Strategic Relationships: How to Extend Your Organization's Reach through Partnerships, Alliances, and Joint Ventures* by William Bergquist, et al. (Jossey-Bass, 1995).

Although supply-chain management has been a recent buzz word, actual supplier and company relations (as opposed to the IT aspects) have received spotty coverage in books. *Balanced Sourcing: Cooperation and Competition in Supplier Relationships* by Timothy M. Laseter (Jossey-Bass, 1998) and *The Connected Corporation: How Leading Companies Win though Customer-Supplier Alliances* (Free Press, 1995) are two that deal with this important area.

Relations between business and the community are addressed mainly in tomes, which include *Community Relations: Unleashing the Power of Corporate Citizenship*, a $495.00, spiral-bound work from the American Productivity & Quality Center, and Edmund M. Burke's *Corporate Community Relations* ($55.00, hardcover; $19.95 paper).

Finally, relations with the media are covered in books on public relations, of which there are many, ranging from the weighty *Effective Public Relations* by Scott M. Cutlip and Allen H. Center (Prentice Hall, 1999, $82.67) to the popularly priced paperback *Value-Added Public Relations* by Thomas L. Harris (NTC Business Books, 1998).

As noted, and as evidenced by the foregoing market survey, the competition is quite fragmented, and only one book even discusses business relationships beyond a narrowly defined segment, specifically customers and employees.

Where Business Is a Contact Sport *Fits*

To our way of thinking, each book noted above makes the case for *Business Is a Contact Sport*. That's because each of them implicitly leads the general reader to focus on one type of relationship—with customers or employees or shareholders or strategic partners or whomever—at the inevitable expense of others. We believe that the late-1980s/early-1990s downsizing trend, with its tight focus on returns to shareholders, may have created the need for all the books on customer service and employee relations that were released in the mid-to-late 1990s. By then, everyone realized that shareholders had benefited at the expense of customers and employees. Hence the need for books on ways to fix the situation.

Now, however, after reading a stack of the available books on business relationships, a manager or entrepreneur could legitimately ask, "OK, which is it? Where should my focus really be? On employees? Customers? Strategic partners? Or what?" After reading any single book among those covered above, most managers would probably make customers or employees or strategic partners the flavor-of-the-month, then after reading another book, switch flavors the following month.

Our holistic view encompasses all business relationships

because people are people regardless of the role they play with a given company at a given time. In fact, each of us plays multiple roles in business in the span of a single day. Regardless of the role we play, we all want our basic human needs for contact, recognition, affiliation, teamwork, and rewards met. Our needs may change when we change roles, but they don't disappear.

Therefore *Business Is a Contact Sport* views the spectrum of businesses relationships as a single, albeit diverse, portfolio of assets to be actively managed and grown. We show readers how to manage and grow that portfolio, systematically and practically.

About the Authors

Tom Richardson and **Augusto Vidaurreta** developed the principles of Relationship Asset Management during their extraordinarily successful careers as consultants, managers, and partners in various ventures, most notably Systems Consulting Group.

In 1988 the authors left Arthur Andersen Management Consulting and established SCG in Miami. During the next seven years the firm was twice named to *Inc.* magazine's list of the 500 fastest growing companies in the United States (in 1992 and 1994). Profitable in every year of its existence, SCG grew (with no outside capital) from an initial investment of $100, which was used to incorporate the company, to an organization of over 200 employees. In time, the SCG client roster included M&M Mars, Quaker Oats, NYNEX, Bell Atlantic, Federal Express, Blockbuster Entertainment, GE Capital, Ryder System, W.R. Grace, Campbell's Soup, Pillsbury, and Burger King.

SCG's ability to attract and retain blue-chip clients and its dominance in the South Florida and Latin American markets made it a sought-after acquisition target for larger consulting firms. In 1995 Cambridge Technology Partners made Tom and

Augusto an offer they couldn't refuse and acquired SCG in a multimillion stock-swap transaction.

Today, the authors' holdings include major ownership positions in a plastics manufacturer in Dalton, Georgia, a bank in Pembroke Pines, Florida, a commercial art and Web site development house in South Florida, a hotel in Singer Island, Florida, and a restaurant in Miami, Florida. These interests were established in the years when a noncompete agreement with Cambridge Technology Partners was in effect.

When the agreement expired in August 1999, Tom and Augusto founded Entente Investments, a venture-capital/mentor-capital firm that practices and promulgates the principles of Relationship Asset Management. *Business Is a Contact Sport* represents a key element in launching both Entente and Relationship Asset Management.

Tom Richardson served as a senior vice president at Cambridge Technology Group from 1995 to 1997. He is active in various South Florida charities, notably as co-founder of the Hook and Ladder Foundation, which assists the poor and homeless, and as founder of one of the area's most successful charity benefit golf tournaments. Tom holds a BA and an MBA from University of Miami.

Augusto Vidaurreta and his family immigrated from Cuba in 1969. His focus on putting people and relationships first throughout his career in the United States represents the origin of Relationship Asset Management. As vice president of Cambridge Technology Partners with responsibility for Latin America, Augusto explored and developed these concepts further. In 1996, he was an Entrepreneur of the Year award finalist in Florida. A regular lecturer at his alma mater, Augusto holds a BA from Florida International University and an MBA from University of Florida.

About the Writing Collaborator

Tom Gorman, doing business as Content Publishing Services, is a business book developer and author based in Newton, Massachusetts. He developed *TechnoLeverage* by F. Michael Hruby (Amacom, 1998), and, with Dr. Paul Miller, co-authored *Big League Business Thinking: The Heavy Hitter's Guide to Top Managerial Performance* (Prentice Hall, 1994). *Big League Business Thinking* was a main selection of the Newbridge Executive Book Club and that title and *TechnoLeverage* were each selected (from 1,200 annual submissions) for long-form summaries by Soundview Executive Book Summaries.

Under his own name, Tom also wrote *The Complete Idiot's Guide to MBA Basics* (Alpha/Macmillan, 1998), *The Complete Idiot's Almanac of Business Letters and Memos* (1997), and the career book *Multipreneuring* (Fireside/Simon & Schuster, 1996).

Tom Gorman has ghostwritten articles for business publications for book-development clients and his by-lined feature articles have appeared in *Business Marketing Magazine* and *The New York Sunday Times* (business section). He is also the author of several book-length industrial reports on such topics as Japanese innovation, the European Economic Union, and health-care cost containment strategies for businesses.

Tom holds a BA from Fairleigh Dickenson University and an MBA from New York University's Leonard N. Stern School of Business.

Specifications of the Book

Format: *Hardcover*

Length: *65,000 words*

Delivery: *Winter, 2000*

Chapter Summaries

Principle #1
See Relationships as Assets

> *Our first principle is that business relationships are valuable assets and therefore must be managed as such. Here we show that every relationship with every stakeholder is important, and that RAM will enable the reader to manage all those relationships.*

We're here to blow the whistle and call time out! We want you to get yourself and your team into a huddle and hear our warning: Your business may be hemorrhaging assets.

Is this alarm necessary? After all, managers typically track down materials breakage and plug inventory leaks. They quickly put idle equipment and empty office space to use. They rid the shop floor of wasted time and motion. They put a quick stop to fraud, embezzlement, uncollected debts, poor investments, and other financial losses.

Yet they often sit stone still, staring into space as some of their most valuable assets leak out, sit idle, or lose money. The assets in question are the company's *relationships*. So we're sounding an alarm—and presenting a game plan for identifying, evaluating, developing, and enhancing these valuable assets.

Under Principle #1 we show that:

- Many management errors, including Microsoft's winding up in an antitrust suit, arise from failure to see relationships as assets
- Every company stands at the center of a Relationship Web
- Relationship Asset Management harnesses relationships in service of the company's goals.

Develop a Relationship Asset Management Strategy

> *In any sport, teams with a solid strategy will outperform those without one. Yet despite the value of relationships, most businesses don't have a strategy for managing them. Principle #2 helps readers to link relationships with business goals.*

The management teams at Time Warner and America Online spent months developing a plan to merge their two companies, which they announced in March, 2000. They would close the deal in autumn. On May first, because of a contract dispute with Disney, parent company of ABC, Time Warner decided to pull ABC's signal from its cable service to 3.5 million homes. The move angered cable customers, opened doors for satellite competitors, aroused suspicion among politicians, and caught the eye of the Federal Communications Commission, which must approve the Time Life-AOL merger.

In the thirty-six hours before an embarrassed Time Warner restored ABC's signal, the company underwent what was widely labeled a public relations disaster. Actually, it was a relationship management disaster. In its dispute with Disney, Time Warner lost sight of its relationship with numerous key stakeholders—customers, shareholders, advertisers, elected local and federal officials, the FCC, and AOL. Even a cursory knowledge of Relationship Asset Management would have prevented this situation.

With Principle #2 readers learn how to:
- Identify the benefits they can gain—and provide—in every relationship
- Cross-reference business goals and objectives with specific stakeholders
- Use RAM to turbocharge their financial, marketing, and operating strategies.

Principle #3
Create Ownership for Relationships

> *Our first principle is that business relationships are valuable assets and therefore must be managed as such. Here we show that every relationship with every stakeholder is important, and that RAM will enable the reader to manage all those relationships.*

Steve Mucchetti, chief operating officer of San Francisco-based Web integrator Scient Corporation says, "The new bottom line is return on relationships, not return on investment." If that's true—and we believe it is—someone must be responsible for the relationship portfolio and for achieving a return on those assets.

That someone is the chief relationship officer, or CRO. Just as a pitching coach and a hitting coach have their specialties, and a chief financial officer and chief information officer have theirs, the chief relationship officer formulates and helps people execute the Relationship Asset Management strategy. The CRO creates the RAM environment and acts as internal consultant, lobbyist, and coach on management decisions that affect the value of relationship assets. He's responsible for saying, "Here's how our relationships with customers (or suppliers or whomever) will be affected if we do this." It's a key function and it's essential to the success of RAM.

In Principle #3 readers:

- See that having an owner for every relationship creates the authority and accountability necessary for RAM to work
- Discover the qualities and skills needed in a relationship owner
- Learn how a chief relationship officer can create an environment in which every relationship becomes stronger.

Principle #4
Turn Contacts into Connections

> *Winners are defined by what they make of the opportunities available to us all. In doing business, we all come in contact with many organizations and individuals. Principle #4 shows readers how to capitalize on every contact.*

In every organization there are uncountable instances of missed opportunities and undeveloped relationship assets, as illustrated by the following:

- A seasoned loading-dock supervisor who knows the operation inside-out takes early retirement to care for his ailing wife. When he leaves, he's gone, never to be seen or heard from again.
- A reporter does a bang-up job covering the opening of the company's new headquarters. An administrative assistant in the publicity department clips and files the article, but no one follows up with the reporter or her editor.
- At a dinner party, a CEO is impressed by a young dentist who is starting his private practice about a mile from headquarters. The executive enjoyed talking with the dentist, but the contact ends there since the company has no dental plan.
- A local university announces a new course of study in a field closely related to the company's business. Several executives who heard about this discuss it at lunch and agree that it's "interesting," and that's as far as it goes.

These contacts represent potentially rich relationships that we show readers how to ignite.

This Principle helps readers see that:

- Every contact is a potential connection, and making connections takes work
- Various stakeholders have various needs for contact
- Prioritizing relationships enables a business to devote the right amount and type of resources to maintaining contacts and connections

Principle #5
Banish Relationship Killers

> *In sports and in business, a fatal mistake can cost the entire team the game. There are, however, ways to avoid mistakes. This principle cues readers to the social and business errors that can doom a relationship at any stage of its development.*

Rome wasn't built in a day, but it only took a day to burn it down. Similarly, relationship assets developed over years can be lost in an instant. Moreover, many relationships never get a chance to develop because one or more of these killers comes to the table:

- *False expectations:* Openness and clarity about desired wins on both sides represent the best insurance of future satisfaction.
- *Win-lose relationships:* A long-term relationship cannot develop if one party has been set up to lose through a power play or cutthroat behavior.
- *Poor preparation:* Gathering information beforehand forestalls the "clueless" approach. You can only go so far with, "I'm nice guy. You're a nice guy."
- *Poor maintenance:* All relationships demand some form of personal contact. Without it, most stakeholders get that taken-for-granted feeling.
- *Betrayal:* This is the deadliest relationship killer, because trust is the basis of every relationship.

With Principle #5 we:

- Illustrate ways of getting off on the right foot in a business relationship.
- Help readers eliminate attitudes and behaviors that place them "out of bounds" without their even knowing it
- Show readers how to find common ground and fit in anywhere.

Principle #6
Get to Know Your Stakeholders as People

> *Many people look at business associates—employees, customers, suppliers, investors, and so on—as dollar signs. That's hell on relationships, bad for business, and not much fun. This principle highlights the importance of personal relationships in business situations.*

Imagine a purchasing manager and a supplier at courtside, begging their favorite player to launch a three-pointer, yelling for a foul that the ref refuses to see, buying each other beers. Then imagine a phone call between them the following week. One of them has bad news. The supplier sees a price increase coming. Or the purchasing agent needs a rush order. The problem occurs in a different, more personal, context than it otherwise would. In that context, there's greater likelihood that they'll work things out.

Like players on a professional sports team, business people spend time together, work together, and help one another, not out of kindness or even, necessarily, friendship. They do it because they are *stakeholders* in one another's success. Yet usually, the better people know one another, the more smoothly a team functions. This often occurs naturally as shared goals foster close relationships. It occurs even more frequently if you know *how to get to know people*. Sports, cultural, and social events and other off-the-job situations offer great opportunities to learn and practice this valuable skill.

This Principle:

- Illustrates the role of personal relationships in business success
- Shows readers what they need to know about a company or person they are doing business with—or want to do business with
- Demonstrates off-the-job ways of getting to know associates.

Principle #7
See Things from the Stakeholder's Standpoint

> *This principle helps readers craft win-win relationships in a range of ways. While money—earning more and paying less—is almost always a desired win, there are also potential nonmonetary wins in most situations. Here we show how to identify **every** win.*

At SCG, we had no promotional budget, but we knew that letters of recommendation and trade magazine articles would be great sales tools. In negotiating with clients, we knew that they would always ask for a reduction in our fee. We often agreed to that—on the condition that we received things that would cost them nothing but would help us a lot.

So we would reduce our fee a bit *if* when the project was finished and had gone well they would become a spokesperson and a reference for us. We could use their name in our materials. They would write a letter of recommendation, and let us write up a case study. If the project was really interesting, a reporter could get interviews and write it up for publication. (This gave them the added win of publicity for themselves.)

To get our staff on board, we rewarded team members on projects that generated a job letter from the client. If the letter was truly glowing, they received a bonus because we hung those on the wall in our reception area. This effort to get client testimonials and cooperation *as part of our contract* helped us create a wonderful reputation.

With this Principle readers:

- Learn how to gauge the motivations of various stakeholders
- Discover "spoking out," a way to place themselves in a stakeholder's position
- See how to create wins for one stakeholder by enlisting other stakeholders.

Principle #8
Create Active Participation

> *Business is not a spectator sport. If any stakeholder becomes a permanent benchwarmer, the owner of that relationship must get them back in the game. Principle #8 strengthens relationships by actively involving everyone on the Relationship Web in the enterprise.*

When Systems Consulting Group started growing rapidly, we realized our benefits plan was inadequate. We saw it as our employees' benefits plan, so we turned its development over to them. We asked them to come up with a benefit plan that made sense for us as employers as well as for them as employees. In several weeks, they presented us with a plan that gave them better benefits than we had anticipated—at a lower-than-anticipated cost to the company. Best of all, they developed it themselves and therefore had ownership of it.

Many employees (to cite one key stakeholder group) now see control over their work lives as a major win. They want to participate in decisions that affect them on the job. When management can channel that desire in a positive direction, the result will be a stronger bond between employer and employee. The same holds true for other stakeholders: participation makes a stakeholder's stake in the business real.

This Principle shows readers how to:
- Give various stakeholders a genuine stake in the business
- Use adversity to strengthen relationships
- Motivate stakeholders to identify more closely with the organization.

Principle #9
Move into the Win-Win Zone

> *RAM aims to maximize the mutual wins in every relationship, to move every relationship into the win–win zone and, over the long term, keep it there. Principle #9 captures practical ways of doing this across a range of stakeholder groups.*

In the 1980s, a major consumer electronics manufacturer was losing market share in paging equipment, a business it had invented. The company went to its suppliers and requested a ten-percent price cut so it could reduce pager costs and regain lost share. The suppliers couldn't see a win for themselves in this proposal and refused. Then the manufacturer started thinking win-win, revised its proposal, and offered to share its technological advances with the suppliers and split the financial benefits, thus giving them a stake in the growth that management expected.

The suppliers responded as hoped. One division head at a supplier said, "We started on the partnership path together by working on tasks that clearly offered near-term benefits to both firms."

Doesn't this differ from the hardball, price-based negotiating that characterizes most company-supplier relationships?

This Principle demonstrates that:

- Maximizing mutual benefits is the surest route to profitable, long-term relationships
- Creating a win proactively can launch a win-win relationship
- Knowing when to quit a losing relationship saves considerable resources.

Principle #10
When Something Breaks, Fix It Fast

You can't win them all, but by taking proper action when things do go wrong, you can turn most of them around. This Principle enables readers to put slumping relationships back in the winners' circle.

When a relationship gets off track, taking action rather than indulging in anger, blame, or regret can put things right. A good relationship built on mutual wins can usually be saved, particularly if problems are caught and corrected early. The chief relationship officer can be invaluable in this area, as coach or pinch hitter. She has to understand the repair process, guide relationship owners through it, and intervene personally when necessary. The following steps (among others) can help get a relationship back on track:

- *Apologize:* We all do things we wish we hadn't. Yet too many of us are unable to say, "I'm sorry." An apology is a actually a show of strength.
- *Accept apologies:* Graciously accepting an apology means openly acknowledging it at the time of delivery and letting it do its job.
- *Resist retaliation:* It's instinctive to want revenge. It's an instinct best resisted.
- *Rebuild the relationship:* If a relationship is in trouble, don't shy away from contact. Although avoidance may feel more comfortable, it will freeze the relationship where it is. Keep in touch and seek opportunities to reestablish trust.

Putting this Principle into practice entails:

- Recognizing when things are off track, so you can start saving the relationship
- Managing one's emotions, a key Relationship Asset Management skill
- Understanding that it takes time and effort to rebuild a relationship, but it is invariably worth it.

Principle #11
Do Business With Integrity

> *In sports, every team comes to stand for something. In business, a company operated with integrity will stand for something that all stakeholders can be proud of. This chapter examines ways to insure that a company operates with integrity.*

The cases of companies-gone-wrong cited in this book all stem at least in part from failure to treat all stakeholders with integrity. In contrast, widely admired companies, such as Hewlett Packard, Southwest Airlines, Starbucks, and Charles Schwab tend to treat their stakeholders well across the board.

Outback Steakhouses uses a five-page Principles and Beliefs Statement that details "how we handle relationships with everyone we deal with, employees, customers, suppliers, neighbors and so on," according to Kevin Harron, director of operations at Tedesco, a major Outback franchisee. Kevin adds, "Outback is about more than making money. Making money is important, and you see that in their success— going from one restaurant to almost 600 in ten or eleven years. But I believe in more than just pushing product out the door and making money, and so does this company."

This Principle shows that:

- Integrated values, actions, and words generate integrity—and vice versa
- Integrity happens every day, or not at all
- Making and honoring the right organizational commitments will ensure that all stakeholders can be proud of the company.

Principle # 12
Never Forget the Home Team

> *Any book claiming that all relationships are assets would be remiss to exclude off-the-job relationships. We close by exploring how Relationship Asset Management works among family and friends and in our broader personal lives.*

We recently heard a fellow at a party describe a friend of his, an entrepreneur with a technology company, by saying, "He's very successful, but he's not happy." To us this sounded contradictory, so we asked why he wasn't happy. "He's going through his second divorce. His teenage son by his first marriage is in a very bad way." We won't trouble you with the rest of his troubles, because we're sure you've heard similar cases.

Many business people fail to realize that the people most important to their success are those at home. Interviews with scores of managers and entrepreneurs confirm that those who describe themselves as successful and feel the sacrifices they made were worthwhile invariably talk about their families and friends when they discuss their lives.

Business pressures and organizational life make it easy to forget that relationships with family and friends—people who are there regardless of your business—are also valuable assets that need management.

With this final Principle readers:

- Recognize that they must also manage their personal relationships as assets
- Realize that their Relationship Web ultimately includes everyone they know
- See examples of business people who weave a wide, supportive, life-enhancing web of relationships over the course of their lives.

Appendix 2

Resources for Business Book Authors

his Appendix lists sources of information on topics relating to business books and to writing and publishing in general. It also includes a list of business book publishers.

Books...

The following are a mix of classic books on the indicated topic along with a few personal favorites of mine, listed alphabetically by title.

...On Writing:

The Business Writer's Handbook by Charles T. Brusaw, Gerald J. Alred, and Walter E. Oliu (St. Martin's Press)

The Elements of Style by William Strunk Jr. and E.B. White (Allyn & Bacon)

On Writing Well by William Zinsser (Harper Resource)

Revising Business Prose by Richard A. Lanham (Allyn & Bacon)

Style: Toward Clarity & Grace by Joseph M. Williams (University of Chicago Press)

Write to the Top by Deborah Dumaine (Random House)

Writing on Both Sides of the Brain by Henriette Anne Klauser (Harper San Francisco)

...On the Publishing Process and the Industry:
The Book Publishing Industry by Albert N. Greco (Allyn & Bacon)

From Book Idea to Best Seller by Michael Snell and Kim Baker (Prima Publishing)

How to Get Happily Published by Judith Appelbaum (Harper Collins)

How to Write a Book Proposal by Michael Larsen (Writer's Digest Books)

How to Write and Sell Your First Nonfiction Book by Oscar Collier and Frances Spatz Leighton (St. Martin's Press)

Kirsch's Guide to the Book Contract by Jonathan Kirsch (Acrobat Books)

Kirsch's Handbook of Publishing Law by Jonathan Kirsch (Acrobat Books)

...On Literary Agents:

Guide to Literary Agents edited by Donya Dickerson (Writer's Digest Books)

How to Be Your Own Literary Agent by Richard Curtis (Mariner Books)

Literary Agents: The Essential Guide For Writers by Debbie Mayer (Penguin USA)

Literary Agents: What They Do, How They Do It and How to Find & Work with the Right One for You by Michael Larsen (John Wiley & Sons)

...On Book Publicity:

Buzz Your Book by M.J. Rose (PDF [portable document format] download available at www.buzzyour.com)

The Complete Guide to Book Marketing by David Cole (Allworth Press)

The Complete Guide to Book Publicity by Jodee Blanco (Allworth Press)

Guerrilla Marketing for Writers by Jay Conrad Levinson, Richard H. Frishman, and Michael Larson (Writer's Digest Books)

Internet Marketing for Less than $500/Year by Marcia Yudkin (Independent Publishers Group)

1001 Ways to Market Your Books by John Kremer (Open Horizons)

...On Public Speaking:
Getting Started in Speaking, Training or Seminar Consulting by Robert
   W. Bly (John Wiley & Sons)

Money Talks: How to Make a Million as a Speaker by Alan Weiss
   (McGraw-Hill)

Speak and Grow Rich by Dottie Walters and Lilly Walters
   (Prentice Hall)

...On Self-Publishing:
The Complete Guide to Self-Publishing by Tom Ross and Marilyn
   Ross (F&W Publications)

Make Money Self-Publishing by Suzanne P. Thomas (Gemstone
   House Publishing)

The Self-Publishing Manual by Dan Poynter (Para Publishing)

A Simple Guide to Self-Publishing by Mark Ortman (Wise Owl
   Books)

Reference Books:
Most of these books are updated annually, and most include articles
of interest, particularly to authors who are new to book publishing.

Guide to Literary Agents edited by Donya Dickerson (Writer's
   Digest Books)

Literary Market Place edited by R. R. Bowker staff (R. R. Bowker)

Writer's Guide to Book Editors, Publishers and Literary Agents by Jeff Herman (Prima Publishing)

Writer's Market edited by Kristen C. Holm (Writer's Digest Books)

Publishers of Business Books

Most of the following publishers and imprints focus solely or heavily on business books. However, some major houses and imprints, such as Simon & Schuster and its Fireside and Touchstone imprints, publish business titles as part of their general nonfiction lists. Other major houses have imprints dedicated to business titles; for instance, HarperCollins has HarperBusiness. Still other houses are dedicated solely to business books. I have also listed a few publishers of professional/technical books and divisions of larger publishers that issue such books.

Although I have included the largest publishers of business books and virtually all the significant smaller ones, this list cannot be completely current, given the pace of change in the industry. In addition, the turnover in the editorial ranks would render a roster of specific editors out-of-date within months and, for that reason, their names are omitted. I have, however, included a brief comment on each publisher.

For the most current information on these publishers and their lists, visit their Web sites, which most of them now have.

Adams Publishing
Adams Media Corporation
57 Littlefield Street
Holbrook, MA 02343
781-767-0994 Fax: 781-767-0994
www.adamsmedia.com
    Adams publishes nonbusiness titles, but focuses strongly on its

business list, which runs heavily toward career and management how-to with creative packaging. Adams series include *Knock 'Em Dead* career books and *Streetwise* business books.

Alpha Books
Pearson Education
201 West 103rd Street
Indianapolis, IN 46290-1097
800-571-5840
www.idiotsguides.com

Alpha Books, a division of Pearson Education, which in turn is part of **Penguin Putnam Pearson**, publishes the *Complete Idiot's Guides*, which include business, as well as nonbusiness titles. Despite the Web-site address, in addition to the *CIG* series, Alpha also publishes business books on a broad array of popular topics.

AMACOM Books
1601 Broadway
New York, NY
212-586-8100 Fax: 212-903-8083
www.amanet.org/books

AMACOM Books is the publishing arm of the American Management Association. Their list ranges from books for a wide management readership to those for niche audiences on business and professional disciplines and technology topics.

Bantam Doubleday Dell Publishing
1540 Broadway
New York, NY 10036
212-354-6500
www.bbd.com

Under its Doubleday/Currency imprint, Bantam Doubleday Dell (a Random House company) publishes commercial but sophisticated management, leadership, strategy, personal finance, and trend titles.

Bard Press
1515 Capital of Texas Highway
Austin, TX 78746
512-329-8373 Fax: 512-329-6051
www.bardpress.com

Bard publishes only several books a year, all of them business books. They look for very creative packaging, and work closely with authors on marketing their books. Subjects include leadership, marketing, success, and investing. Bard actively tends its backlist.

Berrett-Koehler Publishers
235 Montgomery Street
San Francisco, CA 94104
415-288-0260 Fax: 415-362-2512
www.bkpub.com

Berrett-Koehler stresses business books almost exclusively, with an emphasis on the workplace and leadership. They favor a cutting-edge, humanistic but substantive approach to material. This house maintains a strong commitment to its backlist.

Bloomberg Press
100 Business Park Drive
P.O. Box 888
Princeton, NJ 08542-0888
609-279-3000 Fax: 609-683-7523
www.bloomberg.com/products/bbpress.html

Bloomberg Press (part of the Bloomberg financial information empire) publishes specialized books for brokers, money managers, analysts, traders, business owners, and consultants under its Bloomberg Professional Library imprint. The Bloomberg Personal Bookshelf imprint publishes specialized books for consumers and individual investors on topics such as choosing an HMO and buying life insurance.

Broadway Books
1540 Broadway
New York, NY 10036
212-354-6500 Fax: 212-782-9411
www.broadwaybooks.com

See Random House.

Business McGraw-Hill
2 Penn Plaza
New York, NY 10121
212-904-6096
www.books.mcgraw-hill.com/business/contact.html

See McGraw-Hill.

Butterworth-Heinemann
225 Wildwood Avenue
Woburn, MA 01801
781-904-2500
www.bhusa.com

Butterworth-Heinemann, a division of the UK publisher, issues sophisticated books on specialized topics for managers, professionals, consultants, and students. Areas include marketing and sales, HR management, investments, and corporate finance. They also have an imprint focused on the hospitality, leisure, and tourism industry.

Career Press
3 Tice Road
P.O. Box 685
Franklin Lakes, NJ 07417
201-848-0310
www.careerpress.com

Originally focused on job-search and career books, Career Press has moved beyond its namesake topic area to cover a wide range of how-to books and series for managers, entrepreneurs, and consumers (to whom it targets personal finance books).

Crown Business
201 East 50th Street
New York, NY 10022
212-751-2600
www.randomhouse.com/crown/business

See Random House.

Currency (Doubleday/Currency)
1540 Broadway
New York, NY 10036
212-354-6500
www.forthcoming.com
    See Bantam Doubleday Dell Publishing.

Dearborn Publishing Group, Inc.
155 North Wacker Drive
Chicago, IL 60606-1719
312-836-4400 Fax: 312-836-1021
www.dearborntrade.com
    Dearborn publishes under three imprints: Dearborn Trade:
    personal finance, securities, tax, and small business titles.
    Dearborn Financial Publishing: trade and professional books
    and training materials in finance, real estate, and small busi-
    ness, as well as the *If You're Clueless About* series. Upstart Pub-
    lishing: small business titles. The company's books generally
    aim to help readers acquire a skill in a specific area.

Executive Excellence Publishing
1366 East 1120 South
Provo, UT 84606
800-304-9782 Fax: 801-377-5960
www.eep.com
    Executive Excellence publishes a magazine of the same name,
    as well as *Personal Excellence*. The book division issues titles on
    business topics (and some self-help), with an emphasis on
    leadership, organizational development, and personal effec-
    tiveness.

The Free Press
1230 Avenue of the Americas
New York, NY 10020
212-698-7000 Fax: 212-632-4989

The Free Press, a professional (and college textbook) publishing division of **Simon & Schuster**, regularly publishes titles on specialized business topics for a sophisticated audience and the occasional book for the general business reader.

Fireside
1230 Avenue of the Americas
New York, NY 10020
212-698-7000

See Simon & Schuster.

Griffin Publishing Group
18022 Cowan Street Suite 202
Irvine, CA 92614
949-263-3733 Fax: 949-263-3734
www.griffinpublishing.com

Griffin is a trade publisher with a strong position in education (books for educators, not textbooks) and an interesting business list. Titles range from humanistic, inspirational books on mentoring and leadership, to how-to books on protecting your assets and incorporating in Nevada.

HarperBusiness
10 East 53rd Street
New York, NY 10022-6978
(212) 207-7000
www.harpercollins.com/hc/aboutus/imprints/business.asp

HarperBusiness, the first business imprint established by a

major publisher of trade books (in 1992), is also among the most successful. They seek highly commercial titles aimed at general readers on topics such as management, leadership, trends, and companies. HarperCollins also releases business and professional reference books and career how-to books under the HarperCollins imprint.

Harvard Business School Press
60 Harvard Way
Boston, MA 02163
(617) 495-6700
www.hbsp.harvard.edu
> Harvard Business School Press, the publishing division of Harvard Business School, concentrates on substantive, leading-edge topics, usually grounded in academic discipline or original research. That said, HBS Press has successfully emphasized more commercial (as opposed to academic) titles in recent years. Subject areas include organizational behavior, HR management, finance, marketing, production and operations management, accounting and financial control, business history, and managerial economics.

Industrial Press
200 Madison Avenue
New York, NY 10016
212-889-6330 Fax: 212-545-8327
www.industrialpress.com
> Industrial Press is a professional/technical, not a trade, book publisher. They are included because they cover highly specialized technical, engineering, and business topics geared primarily to readers in a manufacturing environment.

Irwin Professional Publishing
1333 Burr Ridge Parkway
Burr Ridge, IL 60521
800-634-3966 or 708-789-4000

> A professional (as opposed to trade book) division of *McGraw-Hill*, Irwin focuses on accounting, finance, and investing, drilling down into subjects such as fraud prevention, portfolio management, and specific types of securities. They also produce video seminars and other information and training products for companies and financial institutions, which are a large part of their customer base.

Jossey-Bass Publishers
989 Market Street
San Francisco, CA 94103
(415) 433-1740
www.josseybass.com

> Jossey-Bass focuses heavily, although not exclusively, on business titles, leaning toward substantive management how-to, often grounded in research or in translating theory into practice. The Jossey-Bass list includes the *Drucker Foundation Future* series and the *Warren Bennis Executive Briefing* series. Jossey-Bass is now part of *Wiley & Sons*.

Kiplinger Books
1729 H Street
Washington, DC 20006
888-419-0424
www.kiplinger.com/books

> A sister division to those that issue Kiplinger magazine and the Kiplinger newsletters, Kiplinger Books focuses on personal financial management titles for the consumer and busi-

ness person. Topics include retirement planning, tax avoidance, investing, home buying, and financing college, among many others.

McGraw-Hill

2 Penn Plaza

New York, NY 10121

212-904-6096

www.books.mcgraw-hill.com/business/contact.html

Long-established business book publisher McGraw-Hill disbanded its trade-book operation in 1989 to focus on professional and reference books. Now, publishing general business as well as professional and reference titles, M-H has returned to the trade-book arena, notably with its *Business McGraw-Hill* imprint. The house also remains strong in the professional and reference area.

Penguin Putnam Pearson

1330 Avenue of the Americas

New York, NY 10019

212-641-2400

www.pearson.com

Penguin Putnam, part of the Pearson publishing empire, established *Portfolio*, a new business imprint in 2002. Portfolio wants highly commercial business books for the general reader on subjects such as leadership, managing, trends, and companies. Penguin Putnam also publishes business books aimed at large markets under its Viking imprint, which is among the house's general nonfiction imprints.

Perseus Books
11 Cambridge Center
Cambridge, MA 02142
617-555-1212
www.perseuspublishing.com

Now a division of HarperCollins, Perseus has a strong position in business books (as well as science, health, parenting, and general nonfiction). Perseus looks for cutting-edge, exploratory approaches to traditional and emerging business skills and trends, as well as very practical how-to books.

Portfolio
1330 Avenue of the Americas
New York, NY 10019
212-641-2400
www.pearson.com

See Penguin Putnam Pearson.

Prentice Hall
1 Lake Street
Upper Saddle River, NJ 07458
www.prenhall.com/author-guide (trade)
www.phptr.com (professional/technical)
www.phdirect.com (direct-to-consumer)

This long-standing business book and textbook publisher, now part of Pearson, is well established in the trade, professional/technical, and direct-to-consumer areas. As a visit to the relevant Web site listed above will show, PH publishes everything from pop leadership and management books (trade) to accounting and finance books (professional/technical) to reference books and guides for managers seeking help with HR, communication, or other on-the-job situations (direct-to-consumer).

Prima Publishing
3875 Atherton Road
Rocklin, CA 95765
916-632-4400 Fax: 916-632-4405
www.primapublishing.com
> Prima has four divisions: Lifestyles, Prima Health, Computers and Technology, and Entertainment. Business books come under Lifestyles and cover subjects such as leadership, home-based business, network marketing, and women in business.

Random House
299 Park Avenue
New York, NY 10171
212-572-2275 Fax: 212-572-4949
www.randomhouse.com
> Random House, the nation's largest book publisher, publishes business books mainly under the banner of *Crown Business*, a division of Random House and *Currency*, an imprint of Doubleday, which is a division of Random House (see separate Bantam Doubleday listing). The *Broadway* division publishes business books aimed at large audiences as part of its general nonfiction list. All imprints and divisions of Random House seek books and authors with broad commercial appeal.

Simon & Schuster
1230 Avenue of the Americas
New York, NY 10020
212-698-7000
www.simonsays.com

Simon & Schuster publishes general nonfiction, including business books, in its trade division under the Simon & Schuster name and under the *Fireside* and *Touchstone* imprints. Another giant on the order of Random House, S&S seeks highly commercial business and personal finance topics.

Ten Speed Press
P.O. Box 7123
Berkeley, CA 94707
510-559-1600 Fax: 510-524-1052
www.tenspeed.com

Not really a "business book publisher," Ten Speed warrants inclusion as the house that *What Color Is Your Parachute?* built. Ten Speed publishes other career and job-search titles and books on entrepreneurship and spirituality in business, always with a unique point of view (to be expected from the publisher of *Psilocybin Mushrooms of the World*).

Texere
55 East 52nd Street
New York, NY 10055
212-317-5511
www.etexere.com

The US arm of the UK publisher, whose name is derived from the Latin verb "to weave," Texere publishes books on management, economics, technology, finance, and other subject areas by business thinkers and idea-driven authors. This house has a unique point of view—a progressive, somewhat intellectual approach to business that's reflected in their list.

Warner Business
1271 Avenue of the Americas
New York, NY 10020
212-522-7200
www.twbookmark.com/business

> Warner Business is the business book imprint of Warner Books, which is part of AOL Time Warner. Warner hit a grand slam with *Rich Dad, Poor Dad*, and founded a series on the title. This publisher wants commercial, clever-but-solid books on management, personal finance, trends, and companies.

John Wiley & Sons
605 Third Avenue
New York, NY 10158
212-850-6000 Fax: 212-850-8641
www.wiley.com

> A major business book publisher, Wiley & Sons covers a huge range of the category's topics—management, career, small business, real estate, investing, trends, and business reference—from the commercial to the cutting-edge. In 2001, the company acquired the *for Dummies* series, which it now publishes in its Hungry Minds division. Wiley also publishes professional and technical books.

Associations and Organizations
American Society of Journalists and Authors
1501 Broadway Suite 302
New York, NY 10036
212-997-0947
www.asja.org

> The ASJA is open to published writers and focuses on both book authors and magazine writers. They hold an excellent

annual writers' conference in New York for nonmembers as well as members.

The Authors Guild
31 East 28th Street 10th Floor
New York, NY 10016
212-563-5904 Fax: 212-564-8363
www.authorsguild.org

The Authors Guild membership includes published book authors and magazine writers, but focuses a bit more on the needs of book authors than the ASJA. The Guild's legal staff will review a book contract for any member who is about to sign one.

Association of Author's Representatives, Inc.
P.O. Box 237201
Ansonia Station
New York, NY 10003
212-252-3695
www.aar-online.org

AAR is the major professional association of literary agents and maintains a Canon of Ethics that all member agents agree to uphold.

Publishers Marketing Association
627 Aviation Way
Manhattan Beach, CA 90266
310-372-2732 Fax: 310-374-3342
www.pma-online.org

PMA membership tends toward small and self-publishers, although authors, publicists, publishing consultants, and other industry professionals also join. PMA hosts an annual conference geared to small publishers and entrepreneurial authors, which rotates from New York to Los Angeles to Chicago and is open to nonmembers and members.

Book Publicists Who Promote Business Books

These are a few among a number of firms (and freelance publicists) that promote business books. For information contact them directly or, when available, visit their Web sites.

Anita Halton Associates Literary Publicity
66 Levant Street,
San Francisco, CA 94114
415-552-4612 Fax: 415-552-4617
ahapub@aol.com
Contact: Anita Halton

Goldberg McDuffie Communications
444 East Madison Avenue Suite 3300
New York, NY 10022
212-446-5100 Fax: 212-980-5228
www.goldbergmcduffie.com
goldberg@goldbergmcduffie.com
Contact: Lynn Goldberg

Monteiro & Company
120 East 56th Street Suite 1030
New York, NY 10022
212-832-8183 Fax: 212-832-9563
monteiro@dti.net
Contact: Barbara Monteiro

Planned Television Arts
1110 Second Avenue 3rd Floor
New York, NY 10022
212-593-5845 Fax: 212-715-1667
www.ruderfinn.com/pta
fishman@ruderfinn.com
Contact: Rick Frishman

Glossary of Book Publishing Terms

acquisitions editor: an editor responsible for purchasing books for publication. At smaller publishing houses, acquisitions editors may also function as copy editors.

advance: amount paid to the author by the publisher to finance or partially finance the writing of the manuscript. Until the advance is "earned out," the publisher keeps the author's royalties on sales of the book and subsidiary rights.

agent: 1. literary agent representing book authors and playwrights (and occasionally screenwriters) 2. talent agent representing actors, directors, screenwriters, and performers.

artwork: diagrams, illustrations, or photographs for a book or book cover. Any material that is not text. (Also known as "art.")

author's copies: most book contracts stipulate that the publisher will send the author a certain number of copies of his book for free, usually from ten to forty copies.

author's discount: most book contracts stipulate that the author may purchase copies of her book directly from the publisher at a discount, usually fifty percent off the cover price.

backlist: see list.

best seller: a book that has met the sales criteria for inclusion on a list compiled by a publication or organization. Authoritative nationwide lists include those of *Publisher's Weekly*, the *New York Times*, and the *Wall Street Journal*. Best-seller lists often omit certain genres of books, and generally measure the pace of sales rather than total sales.

binding: the process and materials used to attach the pages of a book to its cover. A hardcover (or case-bound) book has the pages stitched together and glued into reinforced covers. A softcover (perfect-bound) book has the pages glued into a paper cover.

blad: a mock-up of an excerpt of a book, usually the cover, table of contents, and first chapter. Blads are used in selling and promoting the book before it is actually printed.

blue lines: proof sheets made on photosensitive paper. (Also see proof sheets.)

blurb: a brief testimonial for the book from a credible person. One or more blurbs should appear on the back cover. Multiple blurbs may take up the first few pages.

book contract: legal agreement between an author and a publisher in which the author agrees to write a manuscript of a certain length on a certain subject by a certain date, and the publisher agrees to publish it and pay the author royalties and, usually, an advance. Terms of the contract govern ownership of the material and subsidiary rights, and other considerations.

book packager: see book producer.

book producer: a business or person who finds or is given a book idea, and hires a writer to develop a manuscript for a publisher. Many book producers also hire designers and oversee the manufacture of the books. Book producers do not finance or distribute books, and thus are not publishers. They work for a fee or royalty or both to produce manuscripts or finished (often illustrated) books for publishers.

book publicist: a publicity professional who brings books and their authors to the attention of reviewers, editors, journalists, and broadcast producers.

bound galleys: galleys are pages produced from the typeset pages of the book before the actual book is printed. Bound galleys (also called "galleys") are perfect-bound versions of the book made up of these pages with a plain cover for prepublication reviewers.

branded book: a book sponsored by, and carrying the name of, a business or other organization, usually to promote the organization, a product, or a point of view.

business book: a trade book covering a business topic, such as management, strategy, investing, or finding a job. Many publishers use the categories business/economics or business/personal finance.

coffee-table book: a book, usually in a large trim size, that prominently features drawings, photographs, or other visual elements.

collaborator: a writing partner or a professional writer working on a book with an expert or a co-author.

co-op advertising: advertising in which a publisher and bookstore share the cost of ads for one or more specific titles.

co-publishing: a book project or publishing venture in which two organizations share the publication expenses.

copy: any text may be referred to as copy, but in book publishing the term usually refers to text on the dust jacket and other promotional text.

copy editing: editing a manuscript for accuracy, clarity, grammar, and punctuation and conforming it to the house style.

copy editor: an editor who does copy editing.

copyright: ownership of a literary work. A work is copyright *protected* when an author creates it. However, it is wise to include the copyright symbol, year, and your name on the document. A copyright is *registered* through a filing procedure with the Copyright Office of the Library of Congress. The contents of the book are copyrighted, but titles cannot be. (Titles can be trademarked.) Currently, individual copyright protection of a work lasts for the life of the author plus 70 years. Corporate copyrights have a term of 95 years. When a copyright expires, the work is in the public domain.

corporate history: a book created for a company to document the people, products, and significant events in the development of the organization.

cover credit: one's name on a book's cover. If there is more than one author, "and" denotes equal or nearly equal billing. (The author listed first is typically more famous or the larger contributor.) "With" and "as told to" denote lower levels of contribution to the content and are given to paid collaborators who have negotiated cover credit.

design: 1. cover design refers to the arrangement of typefaces, colors, graphics, and text on the dust jacket or cover of a book 2. interior or page design refers to the choice of typefaces, format, and paper for the pages of the book.

developmental editing: editing for content, structure, logic, and presentation.

drop: see lay-down.

dust jacket: the removable paper cover on a hardcover book.

editor: professional who engages in and oversees the creative aspects, and certain production and business aspects, of publishing a book.

electronic publishing: distributing a book (or other document) on a CD-ROM or other digital storage medium or through the World Wide Web. (Also see print on demand.)

frontlist: see list.

galleys: see bound galleys.

ghostwriter: a professional writer who writes for others for a fee or percentage of the proceeds, or both, without cover credit.

gift book: 1. a book produced with gift-givers as the primary target market. Often these are illustrated books or coffee-table books. 2. a book produced by a company to give to clients, suppliers, and investors.

hold-back: see reserve for returns.

house style: see style guide.

imprint: name of the publisher or, more commonly, the name of a line of books issued by a publisher. Fireside and HarperBusiness are, respectively, imprints of Simon & Schuster and Harper-Collins.

lay-down: number of initial orders for a book that have been placed with the publisher by book sellers, usually through the publisher's sales force (as in "We expect the lay-down for this title to be about 15,000 copies.")

libel: written defamation of a person or organization.

list: publishers usually issue books in two or three seasons per year. The books to be published over the months of a season are that season's list, as in "the spring list" or "the autumn list." Books introduced that season are the frontlist. Books carried over from earlier seasons are the backlist.

market: 1. the target market for a book 2. the market for a certain genre of book, such as the business book or science fiction market 3. the literary marketplace in its entirety, including publishers, bookstores, distributors, and other participants.

mass market paperback: softcover book in a trim size smaller than a trade paperback's, usually about four and a quarter by six and three quarter inches. These books are sold in discount department stores, convenience stores, drug stores, and airports as well as in bookstores.

media list: a list of editors, journalists, and producers who will be sent press releases and other promotional material.

midlist: the term midlist denotes respectable but not outstanding sales, as in "midlist book" or "midlist author."

net price: the price the publisher actually receives for the books sold to distributors, wholesalers, and book stores, usually around 50 percent of the cover price.

on spec: work performed on a speculative basis, with no upfront payment, in anticipation of payment when the finished product is sold.

out of print: a book no longer issued and stocked by its publisher.

packaging: 1. the way in which an idea for a book and the material itself is presented to editors and eventually to the public. Key elements in packaging include the title, subtitle, table of contents, and the author's platform. 2. book packaging (see book producer).

P&L: profit and loss calculation, as when an editor says, "I'll do the P&L before I go into the editorial meeting." This calculation estimates the profit on a book after all direct expenses and allocated overhead have been deducted from an estimated revenue figure.

paste up: 1. pages designed and ready for the camera 2. the process of readying these pages for the camera. The pasted-up pages (now usually designed in desktop publishing software) are photographed and transferred to a metal or paper plate from which the final pages will be printed.

perfect binding: 1. the process of gluing the stacked pages of a book directly to the spine of its cover 2. the binding itself. Almost all softcover books are perfect bound.

plagiarism: to present the work of another person as one's own or to copy from existing sources without crediting them. Generally, "fair use" of copyrighted material permits a reviewer or writer to quote short passages in reviews or in a new work, as long as they are attributed to the original author and work.

platform: elements that enable an author to promote or sell books: fame, notoriety, loyal fans, media exposure, strong sales of previous books, workshops or speaking engagements where books can be sold, or a well-funded promotion plan for the book.

POD: see print on demand.

PP&B: cost of paper, printing, and binding, as when an editor says, "We estimate PP&B at $3.00 per book." Essentially, these are the costs of manufacturing the book itself.

premium: a book given to customers or prospects to promote a company or a specific product or service.

prepublication: anything that occurs before the publication date, such as prepublication sales or prepublication publicity.

press release: a one- or two-page double-spaced document summarizing a newsworthy aspect of the book to be distributed to newspaper and magazine editors, producers, and other potentially interested parties.

printing: a batch of books to be printed, bound, and distributed at one time. If a book sells well, a first printing of 5,000 may be followed by a second printing of 5,000 and so on. Publishers use short print runs to limit the number of unsold books.

print on demand: process of using computerized storage and digital printing technology to make print runs of several copies, or even a single copy, of a book economically feasible.

print run: the number of books to be manufactured in a specific printing.

production: all aspects of creating the book beyond the writing and editing. Includes page design, cover design, layout, typesetting, proofreading, printing, and binding. A book "goes into production" when the manuscript is complete and acceptable to the editor.

professional/technical book: a book that presents specialized material on a discipline to practitioners of the discipline. These books are issued by a professional/technical book publisher or by a division of a trade publisher, and distributed mainly through direct mail and online bookstores.

proofreader: editorial professional who marks corrections to spelling, grammar, punctuation, and style errors in typeset pages ("proofs").

proofreader's marks: special symbols (listed in most dictionaries) used by proofreaders to indicate corrections to be made to the book, usually by the author or editor.

proof sheets: pages produced from the typeset version of the text for review and correction. "Proofs" show how the pages of the book will actually appear.

proposal: a sales document and development plan for a book. The agent or author sends the proposal to editors who may be interested. If an editor likes a proposal, she uses it to sell her colleagues on publishing the book.

publication date: date on which the availability of the book to the public is announced. The "pub date" is usually about three months after the book is printed and bound and is timed to coincide with vigorous publicity and wide distribution efforts.

public domain: work that can be quoted, reprinted, and otherwise used without permission from the author or the copyright owner because the copyright has expired.

publicity: mentions of a book and its author in the print or broadcast media that are not paid for but instead result from touting the newsworthiness of the book and author to editors and producers.

publisher: 1. a business that finances the production, manufacture, promotion, and distribution of books, newspapers, or periodicals 2. the individual responsible for the business (as opposed to editorial) aspects of a publishing business.

quality paperback: see trade paperback.

query: 1. letter to a literary agent or book editor to prompt interest in a book proposal or manuscript 2. a query letter or pitch letter to a magazine or newspaper editor or to a producer to generate coverage for the book in the form of an article or feature.

remaindered books: books drastically marked down by a bookstore to encourage sales. (Also known as "remainders.")

reserve for returns: a percentage of the author's royalty that the publisher holds back to allow for returns because authors receive no royalties on returned books.

returns: unsold books returned to the publisher for full credit by distributors, wholesalers, and bookstores—an industry custom that began in the 1930s.

royalty: a portion of the revenue generated by the book that is paid to the author, usually biannually or quarterly.

royalty rate: a percentage of the cover price or net receipts paid to the author of the book. Royalty rates usually escalate as unit sales of the book reach certain levels.

sell-through: the number of books purchased by consumers from bookstores and other retailers, as in, "The sell-through looks good so far." If the sell-through is poor, the result is returns.

series: a succession of books issued by a publisher on a topic or related topics under a standard title and in a consistent style of writing and design.

sponsoring editor: see acquisitions editor.

style guide: a document, ranging from a page or two to dozens of pages, that sets forth the publisher's way of writing terms that are matters of style rather than proper usage ("house style"). Many style guides also suggest approaches to writing for the publisher's audience.

subsidiary rights: rights to use content from the book in other revenue-generating forms. Key "sub rights" for business books are foreign language rights, electronic rights, and audiobook rights.

subsidy press: a business that charges authors to produce and manufacture their books. Typically, subsidy presses provide no promotion or distribution and do not publish books of trade-book quality.

trade book: a book published for and distributed to general readers through traditional and online bookstores, as well as other sales channels, such as gift shops and department stores, and libraries. (Compare with professional/technical book.)

trade paperback: a softcover book in a hardcover trim size or larger, usually priced between $10 and $20.

trim size: the size of the pages of the book. For hardcover business books, the trim size is usually six by nine or five-and-a-half by eight-and-a-half inches.

vanity press: see subsidy press

Index

to agents, 59–60
definition of, 283
to publications, 184–187
to radio and television producers, 187–188
sample, 59, 185
Quotes, humorous, 150–151
Quoting
articles, 87
facts and figures, 148–149
statistics, 87

R
Radio producers, query letters to,
187–188
RAM. *See* Relationship Asset
Management
Random House, 266
Readers. *See* Audience
Real estate investing guides, 15
Reference books, 254–255
Relationship Asset Management
(RAM), 43
Remaindered books, 283
Repackaging material, 35–36
Reprints, 187
Research, 6
on agents, 55–58
for competitive analysis, 91–96
for examples and cases, 143–144
for ideas, 38–39
on publishers and editors, 58
before writing, 134–135
Reserve for returns, 283
Returns, 283
Review copies, 183–184
Richardson, Tom, 43, 215
Ringer, Robert, 2
Robbins, Harold, 123

Roberts, Wess, 6
Rockefeller, John D., Sr., 43–44
Rose, M. J., 194
Rosenthal, Morris, 194
Royalty, 29, 53, 284
Royalty rate, 67, 284

S
Sales, books on, 11–12
Sample chapter, 123–130
Schedule
for promotion, 203–206
for writing, 134–136
Schlosser, Eric, 42
"Season," 21–22
Second Careers (Bird), 96
Security, need for, 40–41
Self-help books. *See* Business how-
to/self-help books
Self-publishing, 23–25, 194, 254
Self-Publishing Manual (Poynter), 25
Sell-through, 284
Sentence length, 138–139
Series, 19–20, 284
Service firms, developing books,
35–36
*The Seven Habits of Highly Effective
People* (Covey), 5, 36, 46,
108–110, 145
*The 75 Greatest Management Decisions
Ever Made* (Crainer), 147
"Shakedown cruise," 125
Shifting Gears (O'Neill), 96
Similes, 145–146
Simon & Schuster, 266–267
Slang terms, 48
Small-office/home-office (SOHO),
books on, 13
Small publishers, 22–23